STECK-VAUGHN SOCIA

Homes and Families

Teacher's Guide

Level A

ISBN 0-8172-6556-2

Copyright © 1997 Steck-Vaughn Company.
Steck-Vaughn Company grants you permission to duplicate
enough copies of blackline masters to distribute to your
students. All other material contained in this publication
may not be reproduced in whole or in part without
permission in writing from the copyright owner. Requests
for permission to make copies of any part of the work
should be mailed to: Copyright Permissions, Steck-Vaughn
Company, P.O. Box 26015, Austin, Texas 78755. Printed in
the United States of America.

3 4 5 6 7 8 9 BP 01 00 99

STECK-VAUGHN
C O M P A N Y
ELEMENTARY • SECONDARY • ADULT • LIBRARY

ACKNOWLEDGMENTS

Executive Editor: Diane Sharpe

Project Editor: Janet Jerzycki

Assistant Art Director: Cynthia Ellis

Design Manager: John J. Harrison

Program Development, Design, Illustration, and Production: Proof Positive/Farrowlyne Associates, Inc.

Contents

The Philosophy of Steck-Vaughn Social Studies

Social studies focuses on developing knowledge and skill in history, geography, anthropology, economics, and political science. Most importantly, it focuses on people and their interaction with each other and the world in which they live. *Steck-Vaughn Social Studies* addresses these areas of study in a six-level program that correlates with the social studies curriculum throughout the United States. This program can serve as an alternative to traditional basal textbooks. *Steck-Vaughn Social Studies* helps students acquire the skills, knowledge, and understanding they must have in order to function as concerned and involved members of our society.

Steck-Vaughn Social Studies is a program that both you and your students will enjoy using. Its approach is based on widening the horizons of students as they progress through the elementary grades. Students will gain a concrete, understandable framework for learning the principles of democracy and citizenship. They will also gain a better vantage point from which to view the world's diversity.

ABOUT THE PUPIL EDITIONS

The individual features of *Steck-Vaughn Social Studies* have been designed to help students meet with success in their study of social studies. A variety of features work together to create books that are both inviting and manageable for students who have difficulty reading in this content area.

Format

The pupil texts are divided into units and chapters of manageable length. Each unit opener identifies the important concepts of the unit and sets the stage for successful reading by asking questions to spark student interest. A photograph welcomes students to each new unit. The unit opener also suggests an idea for an appealing cooperative learning project for students to carry out as they read the unit. The unit closes with suggestions of ways students can complete and present their project.

Interactive Activities

Activities on the pupil edition pages ensure student involvement by asking them to respond to the text. Many of the activities emphasize geography skills. Activities also include recall questions, higher-level thinking questions, and activities that require student interaction with maps, charts, and illustrations.

Readability

A readable and manageable text draws students into the content and ensures their understanding. The text never talks down to students or overwhelms them, but rather respects them and presents the content in a form they will understand and enjoy. Difficult concepts are presented in a straightforward manner. The students' prior knowledge is used as a starting point for presenting new concepts. The reading level is carefully controlled at or below grade level in order to ease the difficulties students often have with reading content-area materials.

Text	Reading Level
Level A	Grade 1
Level B	Grade 2
Level C	Grade 2
Level D	Grade 3
Level E	Grade 3
Level F	Grade 4

Vocabulary

Key social studies terms are boldfaced and defined in context in the texts. The glossary at the end of each book lists the terms and their definitions alphabetically.

Special Feature Pages

These pages appear at the end of every chapter and focus on a person, place, or event that extends the chapter content. For example, "Around the Globe" special features in Level C take students to Australia and Canada. In the chapter about ancient Egypt in Level F, the "Special People" feature focuses on Hatshepsut. One "For Your Information" in Level E extends the content of the Civil War with a description of the Freedmen's Bureau set up to help African Americans after the war.

History Strand

Steck-Vaughn Social Studies addresses the often neglected need for history in the lower grades. For example, students at Level A read about the first families in the United States—American Indians and Pilgrims. At Level C, students explore the development of a community—Omaha, Nebraska—from the days of the Omaha people to the present.

Skills Program

Each unit includes social studies and geography skills such as maps, globes, charts, and graphs as part of its narrative content. A Skill Builder at the end of each unit extends the content, at the same time reviewing a social studies or geography skill taught previously in the unit.

Maps and Illustrations

Students are drawn into the texts by abundant maps and illustrations that enhance their understanding of the content.

Chapter Checkups

Checkup tests provide successful closure to each chapter. The consistent format helps students feel comfortable in a review situation. Each Checkup consists of questions in standardized test format, which address the factual content of the chapter. A critical-thinking-and-writing question that requires students to display their deeper understanding of a chapter concept concludes the chapter.

ABOUT THE TEACHER'S GUIDE

The separate Teacher's Guide presents strategies for units and chapters with guidelines and answers for the interactive text; mid-term and final tests; letters to families; and useful graphic organizers.

Teaching Strategies

The unit strategies include a unit summary, pre- and post-reading activities, guidelines for implementing the unit project, and bibliographies for both teacher and student. In addition, references to the Teacher's Resource Binder blacklines are included, should you choose to purchase this additional resource.

The chapter strategies include activities for pre- and post-reading, as well as a chapter summary, objectives, a list of vocabulary along with vocabulary activities, and page-by-page teaching suggestions and answers to interactive text.

These activities can help teachers accommodate the individual and group needs of students.

Letters to Families

Family letters are provided for every unit of Levels A, B, C, and D, and for each book of Levels E and F. The letters invite families to participate in their child's study of the book and provide suggestions for some specific activities that can extend the concepts. A separate Spanish version of each letter is also provided.

Assessment and Evaluation

A mid-term and final test are provided in the Teacher's Guides for Levels C, D, E, and F. The tests are in the standardized test format familiar to students from the Chapter Checkups.

To implement portfolio assessment, invite students to select samples of their best work to supply for their portfolios. Ask them to tell you which work they are most proud of and why. You may want to suggest that students' work on the cooperative learning unit projects be considered for their portfolios. Allow students to discuss with you any work they would like to change and how they would change it.

CONTENT SCOPE AND SEQUENCE

	LEVEL A	LEVEL B	LEVEL C
HISTORY	• People, families, and neighborhoods change over time. • American Indians were the first Americans. American Indians helped the Pilgrims to survive. • National holidays and patriotic symbols remind us of our heritage.	• American Indians were the first Americans. • Christopher Columbus came to America in search of new trade routes. • American Indians helped the Pilgrims survive in America. • Neighborhoods change over time. • Holidays commemorate special events and people from our history.	• American Indians made up our nation's earliest communities. • Pioneers settled on American Indian land and built communities such as Omaha, Nebraska. • Thanksgiving celebrates an event in American history. • Each community has its own history that we can research.
GEOGRAPHY	• Families live in homes of different sizes and shapes. • Different families need or want to live in different places (near rivers, mountains, etc.). • A globe is a model of Earth. • Earth provides us with many resources.	• Neighborhoods are real places we can show on maps. • Globes are ways of showing the whole, round Earth. • Neighborhoods around the world are both alike and different. • There are seven continents on Earth. • Earth has different geographic features such as mountains, plains, rivers, and oceans.	• Life in communities often depends on natural resources, climate, and landforms. • Water is a very valuable natural resource. • Plains and mountains are important landforms. • The American Indian way of life was shaped by the land.
GOVERNMENT/ CITIZENSHIP	• Rules help us to live, work, and play at home and in the community. • We have responsibilities in our families. • Families share feelings about their country and about their flag. • It is important to take care of the environment. • Families remember great Americans and events on special days.	• We live in the United States of America. • Neighbors work together to solve mutual problems. • Rules and laws tell us what to do and what not to do. Rules and laws help us live together. • Groups have leaders (mayor, governor, President).	• A community is run by a government. • Government leaders are elected by the people of a community. • Communities have laws to tell people what to do and how to act, to protect people, and to provide safety. • Our national government is based in Washington, D.C.
ECONOMICS	• People work to earn money to buy the things they need and want. • Some people produce goods and others provide services. • We can't always have everything we want. People make choices as to which needs and wants they will satisfy.	• Some people produce goods and others provide services. • Workers cooperate to produce goods. • People use the money they earn to buy the things they need and want. • The choice of jobs may be limited by the place in which a person lives. • Taxes help pay for many community services.	• As workers, people are producers; as buyers, they are consumers. • One product may be produced by many people working in different communities. • Communities depend on one another. • Jobs and industry determine whether or not a community will grow or shrink.
SOCIOLOGY/ ANTHROPOLOGY	• Families vary in size and structure. • Families provide for physical and emotional needs and wants. Different families have somewhat different rules and private holidays. • Schools are special places for learning. • All family members can help the family meet its needs and wants.	• Neighborhoods are places in which to live, work, and play. • Neighbors vary in age, language, and other human characteristics. • People share the customs of their homelands with new friends and neighbors in the United States. • Neighbors share local and national holidays.	• Communities vary in size: rural towns, suburbs, and cities. • People live, work, and play in communities. • Living in communities makes it easier to get things done and to help people. • We have American traditions. • We also have many individual family traditions.

CONTENT SCOPE AND SEQUENCE

	LEVEL D	LEVEL E	LEVEL F
HISTORY	• The American Indians were the first to settle in what is now the U.S. • The U.S. has always been a nation of immigrants. • The geography and natural features of a region affect the course of its history.	• The history of the U.S. tells how different groups built a strong nation. • U.S. history can be divided into several distinct periods. • The study of these periods shows how people and events have shaped the present. • The study of the past shows the development of important ideas.	• Civilizations in Asia, Africa, Europe, and the Americas made key contributions to human life and knowledge. • The ancient Greeks and Romans and the nations of Western Europe have influenced many nations. • Geography, trade, and technology can affect the development of a civilization.
GEOGRAPHY	• The U.S. is a large nation. It includes 50 states and Puerto Rico. • The Northeast, Southeast, North Central, Rocky Mountain, Southwest, and Pacific regions are groups of states with characteristic geographic features. • Landforms and climate influence the way people live and work.	• The U.S. has diverse landforms, climates, and natural resources. • The U.S. can be divided into several distinct regions. • The geography of the U.S. has affected the ways in which the nation was explored and settled. • U.S. geography has influenced economic activities.	• Varied land regions, climates, resources, and bodies of water are found on Earth. • People adapt differently to different natural environments. • Latitude, altitude, and ocean currents can affect climate. Climate affects cultures. • A wise use of resources is necessary for a healthy environment.
GOVERNMENT/ CITIZENSHIP	• The U.S. is a democracy in which voters are free to choose their leaders in local, state, and national governments. • Each level of government handles different kinds of problems and functions. • Americans share pride in a heritage they have built together.	• The U.S. is a democracy. • The U.S. Constitution contains the beliefs of the colonists about freedom, equality, justice, and property. • It establishes the branches of the government. • The Constitution (including the Bill of Rights) has been the basis for the rights of Americans.	• Governments vary from dictatorships to democracies. • Ancient Greek and Roman governments influenced our own. • The roles of citizens can vary from no participation to making many political choices. • Economic upheavals and new political ideas can change government.
ECONOMICS	• Americans do many jobs that are created by the U.S.'s wealth, natural and human resources, education, and freedom to make choices as interdependent consumers and producers. • Transportation and communications systems allow the exchange of goods and materials produced in different places.	• Americans have several ways of acquiring goods, services, and property. • Natural resources and technology have influenced economic activities in different U.S. regions. • Changes in transportation and communication have affected economic activities.	• Nations trade with one another to obtain needed raw materials and goods. • Economic development is affected by a nation's government, resources, technology, trade policies, and trade practices.
SOCIOLOGY/ ANTHROPOLOGY	• Individual Americans, though diverse in occupation, family heritage, and other human characteristics, share certain American customs, languages, and symbols.	• American Indians had developed cultures before the arrival of European settlers. • Different groups have made contributions to U.S. society. • American traditions influence our approach to issues such as minority rights and conservation of resources.	• The values and beliefs of a culture influence its growth and development. • The culture of a society includes its customs and religious beliefs. • Advanced cultures have writing, art and architecture, science, and mathematics. • Trade and war can lead to the diffusion of cultures and to new cultures.

SKILLS SCOPE AND SEQUENCE

	LEVELS:	A	B	C	D	E	F
GEOGRAPHY AND OTHER SOCIAL STUDIES SKILLS	Understanding globes	8	4	8	14		2, 12, 18
	Understanding time zones						1, 17
	Using map keys	7	1, 4, 9	1, 2, 12	1, 4, 6, 8, 10, 12, 13	3, 4, 5, 6, 8, 10, 11, 13, 14, 16, 17	2, 4, 7, 8, 10, 14, 19, 20
	Using scale and distance			1, 2, 12	4, 5, 10, 11, 14	2, 5	6, 9, 15, 16
	Working with directions	6, 7, 8, 9, 10	1, 4, 9, 11	1, 2, 3, 4, 5, 6	1, 4, 6, 7, 8, 10, 12, 13, 15	2, 8, 9	9
	Working with landforms	8	1, 5	2, 5	1, 4, 5, 7, 8, 9, 10, 11, 12	2, 17	2, 12, 16, 17, 18
	Working with latitude and longitude						2, 12, 16
	Working with maps	7, 8, 9	1, 4, 9, 10, 11	1, 2, 3, 4, 5, 6, 10, 11, 12, 13, 14	1, 2, 4, 5, 6, 7, 8, 9, 10, 11, 12, 13, 14	1, 2, 3, 4, 5, 6, 8, 9, 10, 11, 13, 14, 16, 17	1, 2, 3, 4, 5, 6, 7, 8, 9, 10, 11, 12, 13, 14, 15, 16, 17, 18, 19, 20
	Working with graphs	6	5, 7	9, 11	2, 3, 11	11, 12, 14	15, 16
	Working with time lines		12	13	13, 15	2, 5, 6	9
	Working with charts	11	3, 9	9, 11	7	2, 4, 7	6, 10
	Working with diagrams			8, 12, 15	3, 14		
	Working with tables				6		
THEMATIC STRANDS IN SOCIAL STUDIES	Culture	1, 2, 3, 4, 5, 6, 7, 8, 9, 10, 11, 12	1, 3, 4, 5, 6, 7, 8, 9, 10, 11, 12	1, 2, 3, 4, 5, 6, 7, 8, 9, 10, 11, 12, 13, 14, 15, 16	1, 2, 3, 5, 6, 7, 9, 10, 11, 12, 13, 14, 15	1, 2, 3, 4, 5, 6, 7, 8, 9, 10, 11, 12, 13, 14, 15, 16, 17, 18	1, 2, 4, 5, 6, 7, 8, 9, 10, 11, 13, 14, 15, 16, 17, 19, 20
	Time, continuity, and change	1, 4, 6, 7, 9, 10, 11, 12	2, 3, 4, 10	1, 3, 6, 9, 12, 13, 14, 15, 16	2, 3, 5, 7, 8, 9, 10, 11, 13, 14, 15	1, 2, 3, 4, 5, 6, 7, 8, 9, 10, 11, 12, 13, 14, 15, 16, 17, 18	1, 4, 5, 6, 7, 8, 9, 10, 11, 13, 14, 15, 16, 17, 18, 19, 20
	People, places, and environments	1, 2, 3, 4, 5, 6, 7, 8, 9, 10, 11, 12	1, 2, 3, 4, 5, 6, 7, 8, 9, 10, 11	1, 2, 3, 4, 5, 6, 7, 8, 9, 10, 11, 12, 13, 14, 15, 16	1, 2, 3, 5, 6, 7, 8, 9, 10, 11, 12, 13, 14, 15	1, 2, 3, 4, 5, 6, 7, 8, 9, 10, 11, 12, 13, 14, 15, 16, 17, 18	1, 2, 3, 4, 5, 6, 7, 8, 9, 10, 11, 12, 13, 14, 15, 16, 17, 18, 19, 20
	Individual development and identity	1, 2, 3, 6, 7, 8, 9, 10, 11, 12	4, 6, 7, 8, 9, 10, 11, 12	1, 3, 4, 5, 6, 8, 9, 10, 11, 12, 13, 14, 15, 16	2, 3, 4, 7, 9, 11, 13, 14, 15	1, 3, 4, 5, 6, 7, 8, 9, 10, 11, 12, 13, 14, 15, 16, 17, 18	4, 5, 6, 7, 8, 9, 10, 11, 13, 14, 15, 16, 19, 20
	Individuals, groups, and institutions	1, 2, 3, 4, 5, 6, 7, 8, 9, 10, 11, 12	1, 2, 3, 4, 5, 6, 7, 8, 9, 10, 11, 12	1, 3, 4, 6, 7, 9, 10, 11, 12, 13, 14, 15, 16	3, 4, 5, 6, 9, 10, 11, 12, 13, 14, 15	1, 2, 3, 4, 5, 6, 7, 8, 9, 10, 11, 12, 13, 14, 15, 16, 17, 18	1, 4, 5, 6, 7, 8, 9, 10, 11, 13, 14, 15, 16, 17, 19, 20
	Power, authority, and governance	1, 2, 3, 4, 5, 6, 7, 8, 9, 12	6, 7, 8, 9, 10, 11	1, 2, 3, 7, 9, 10, 11, 12, 14, 15, 16	3, 7, 9, 11, 13, 15	3, 4, 5, 6, 7, 8, 9, 10, 11, 12, 13, 14, 15, 16, 17, 18	1, 4, 5, 6, 7, 8, 9, 10, 11, 13, 14, 15, 16, 17, 19, 20
	Production, distribution, and consumption	3, 4, 5, 8, 10, 11	3, 4, 5, 6, 7, 9	1, 3, 5, 7, 8, 12, 13, 14	5, 6, 7, 8, 9, 11, 12, 13, 15	1, 3, 4, 5, 9, 10, 11, 12, 13, 14, 15, 16, 17, 18	1, 3, 4, 5, 6, 7, 8, 10, 11, 12, 13, 14, 15, 16, 17, 19
	Science, technology, and society	1, 4, 5, 7, 9	2, 5, 7, 10	1, 4, 7, 8, 10, 13, 14	1, 7, 9, 13, 14, 15	2, 3, 10, 11, 12, 13, 14, 15, 16, 17, 18	1, 3, 4, 5, 6, 8, 9, 10, 11, 13, 14, 15, 16, 18, 20
	Global connections	2, 3, 6, 8, 9, 12	1, 3, 4, 5, 10, 11, 12	5, 6, 8, 11, 16	2, 4, 5, 6, 7, 8, 10, 12, 14, 15	1, 2, 3, 5, 6, 10, 12, 15, 16, 17, 18	1, 2, 3, 4, 6, 7, 8, 9, 10, 11, 13, 14, 16, 17, 19
	Civic ideals and practice	4, 5, 6, 7, 9, 12	4, 5, 7, 8, 9, 10, 11, 12	1, 3, 7, 8, 9, 10, 11, 12, 13, 14, 15, 16	3, 4, 7, 9, 13	3, 4, 5, 6, 7, 10, 11, 12, 15, 17, 18	3, 4, 5, 6, 8, 9, 10, 11, 15, 16

Unit Summary Families vary in size and structure. They provide for both the physical and emotional needs of their members. Family members share many things, such as household chores, vacations, and ways of doing things. They work and play together.

Before Reading the Unit Show students pictures of various animal families, such as birds in a nest or a dog with her puppies. Discuss how we know these groups are families. Which animal is the parent? How many babies are in the picture? How do the animal parents care for the babies?

Tell students they will learn about human families in this unit. Ask them to look at the photograph on the unit opener on page 5. Ask students what this picture shows a family doing. Have students read the questions. Tell them to look for answers to these questions as they read Unit 1.

Point out the Unit Project box and read the assignment with students. Explain that they will work on this project as they read the unit.

Unit Project

Setting Up the Project Prepare for this project by bringing to class a variety of magazines containing pictures of different kinds of families for students to cut out.

Students will find specific suggestions in the Project Tip sections of the chapters. Encourage them to adapt the suggestions to their own interests that are pertinent to the chapter topics.

Presenting the Project Students can use one of the suggestions on page 22 to share and present their project, or they can choose another way. One alternative is for each student to make a family poster. They can paste their family pictures on a piece of poster board, then draw pictures showing different ways their family lives, works, and plays together.

After Reading the Unit Invite discussion of the unit opener questions. Prompt further discussion by asking such questions as: How is your family like the families you read about? How does your family help you? How do you help other members of your family? Why do families need rules?

Skill Builder

Learning About Alike and Different

Before students read page 21, review the concepts of alike and different, emphasizing that although families can be very different, they can also be alike. Invite students to give examples of families they know who are both different and alike. Then have them read the Skill Builder and write their answers.

Answers: Students should tell how families are alike by putting a checkmark next to the sentence *Families help us.* They should tell how families are different by putting a checkmark next to the sentence *Families are large or small.*

Bibliography

Teacher

Cohen, Elizabeth G. *Designing Groupwork.* 2nd edition, Teacher's College Press, 1994.

Ellis, A. K. *Teaching and Learning Elementary Social Studies.* 4th edition, Allyn & Bacon, 1991.

Johnson, David W. and Roger T. Johnson. *Learning Together and Alone.* 4th edition, Prentice-Hall, 1994.

Stahl, Robert J. and Ronald L. Van Sickle (eds.). *Cooperative Learning in the Social Studies Classroom.* National Council for the Social Studies, 1992.

Student

Auster, Benjamin. *I Like It When.* (Ready • Set • Read Series) Steck-Vaughn, 1992. (Grade 1)

Goldish, Meish. *The Same But Different.* (Real Reading Series) Steck-Vaughn, 1989. (Grades 1–2)

Haskins, Francine. *Things I Like About Grandma.* Children's Book Press, 1992. (Grades 2–3)

Hulbert, Jay and Kantor, Sid. *Armando Asked, "Why?"* (Ready • Set • Read Series) Steck-Vaughn, 1992. (Grade 1)

Magnetic Way Thematic Activity Modules. *My Family and Me.* [*Mi Familia y Yo.* (Spanish version)] Steck-Vaughn, 1994. (Grades PreK–1)

Teacher's Resource Binder

Blackline Masters for Unit 1: Unit 1 Project Organizer, Unit 1 Review, Unit 1 Test; Activities for Chapters 1, 2

Chapter Summary Although there are big families and small families, all families are alike in many ways. Families give each other love, help, and safety. Families also change. They grow, they move, parents change jobs, and children change schools.

Chapter Objectives Students will learn to

- recognize how family members help each other.

- identify the ways in which families change.

Vocabulary
family, p. 6

Vocabulary Activities Show students a flashcard displaying the word *family*. Read the flashcard aloud, and discuss what the word means. Tack the card on the bulletin board. Ask students to dictate sentences that tell what they know about families. Write each student's sentence on chart paper as it is dictated. Then read the sentences, and ask students to find the word *family* in the sentences. Underline the word each time it is found.

Before Reading the Chapter Point out that many of the people with whom we live have the same last name that we have. Other people in our household may look like us or like one another. Ask students to tell why they think many family members share a last name and look alike. Show pictures of various adult animals. Next show pictures of young animals (same breed and species as the adults). Have students match the pictures of the young animals with the older parents. Discuss how students were able to match the animals.

Teaching Suggestions and Answers
Page 6
Discuss the meaning of the words *large* and *small*. How are large and small families alike? (Possible answers: all families need food, clothing, a place to live.) How are large and small families

different? (Possible answers: large families might be noisier than smaller families; their homes might be larger and more crowded.) **Students should circle the picture of the large family at the bottom of the page. They should put a blue checkmark next to the picture of the small family.**

Page 7
Discuss what it means to be a large or a small family. Ask students: How many people are in a large family? How many are in a small family? (Answers will vary.) Ask students to tell about their families. Ask students to tell if their families are large or small. Then ask students to tell what they like about being a member of a small or large family. Have them model the activity in the book by drawing pictures of their families. **Student drawings will vary.** Encourage students to share their pictures with the class and to identify each family member.

Page 8
Discuss what it means to help someone. Ask students: Who helps you at home? Whom do you help? (Answers will vary.) Then ask students how people in their family show their love. **Students should draw a circle around the man in the photograph. They should draw a line under the girl in the photograph. Students should write the name of someone who helps them at home. Answers will vary.**

Page 9
Discuss ways that our families help us. Invite students to tell ways that their families help them. Possible answers include giving them food, caring for them when they are sick, loving them, buying them clothes, playing games with them and spending time together, helping them with homework, and so on. Discuss the pictures with students. Ask them how these pictures show families helping. **Students should put a red checkmark next to the photograph of the family shopping for food. They should put a green checkmark next to the picture of the person making clothes.**

Page 10

Explain that families do not stay the same. Family members grow older. Sometimes families grow larger, and sometimes they get smaller. Discuss the kinds of changes that happen when people marry, babies are born, grandparents move in with families, parents divorce, older brothers and sisters move out, and so on. Encourage volunteers to give examples of how their families have changed. What was it like? How did you feel starting a new school? Have students look at the pictures. Point out that these are pitures of the same family at different times. Discuss what is happening in the pictures. **Students should number the pictures in the correct time sequence.**

Page 11

Discuss other ways in which families change. Ask students if any of them have ever moved or changed schools. Ask them to describe the experience. What was it like? How did you feel starting a new school? Have students look at the pictures. **Students should put a checkmark over the photograph of the family moving.**

Project Tip

Call students' attention to the Project Tip and discuss the suggestion. Tell students to explain to their parents why they want the pictures and to ask their parents to tell them about the family photographs.

Page 12

Special People You might tell students that Gwendolyn Brooks was born in Topeka, Kansas, and moved to Chicago when she was a small girl. It was one of the first big changes in her life. In her poems and other writings, she talks about changes and experiences she went through as a child. Explain to students that a poem is a group of words that are written in lines that have a rhythm. Often, a poem also rhymes. Explain to students that Brooks was the first African American poet to win the prestigious Pulitzer Prize. You might wish to read aloud a few of Brooks's poems from her book, *Bronzeville Boys and Girls*, Harper, 1956. "Bronzeville" is the name of the neighborhood in Chicago where Brooks grew up. **Student answers will vary, but they should respond by telling something they would write about being**

in a family. **Encourage students to discuss their answers.**

Page 13

Technology Discuss with students why families do not always live together. Emphasize that even though there are reasons they must be apart, they still care about each other. Discuss how family members can keep in touch. Have students look at the pictures and discuss the technology that each picture shows. You might ask students to tell other ways their family uses to keep in touch. (Possible answers might include: fax and audio or video recordings.) **Students should put a checkmark beside the picture of each form of communication that their family uses.**

Page 14

Chapter Checkup You may want to work through the Chapter Checkup with students. Make sure they all understand what the correct answers are.

Answers: Students should circle the picture of the family at the museum. Students should draw a line over the two oldest people and put an *X* over the picture of the youngest girl.

Encourage several students to share their ideas. Possible answers include: a child is born; a child is adopted; a family moves.

After Reading the Chapter

Have students make a class collage entitled "How Families Help Us." Using magazines, have students cut out pictures of food, homes, clothing, and other things that families use to help each other. Have them paste the pictures on poster board or chart paper. This can be an ongoing project.

Writing

Have students write a letter to parents or guardians thanking them for something they have done to help them.

Literature

Have students write short poems about their families. Help students by sharing short poems with them before they begin writing. Explain that their poems do not have to rhyme and do not have to be longer than several lines.

Chapter Summary Families both work and play together. They work at home to help each other. They play together at home and in other places. Families also have rules that help them live together. There are clean-up rules, safety rules, and bedtime rules.

Chapter Objectives Students will learn to

* identify the activities families do together.

* identify the meaning of a rule, as well as the necessity for rules.

* tell the ways families are the same and different, no matter where they live.

Vocabulary

rules, p. 17

Vocabulary Activities Ask each student to give his or her own definition of the word *rules*. Ask them to tell how rules might help us. Help students categorize rules as school rules, bedtime rules, safety rules, and so on.

Before Reading the Chapter Display a picture of a very messy room that the whole family might use, such as a kitchen. Ask students to tell what needs to be done to make the room clean. Ask each student to identify one job that must be done to achieve this end. Suggestions may include picking up toys, or washing the dishes and mopping the floor. Record student answers on chart paper. As an alternative, have students make a picture of an activity they like to do at home. Then have them make a picture of an activity they like to do away from home, such as going to the movies or playing with a friend.

Teaching Suggestions and Answers
Page 15
Discuss the jobs that need to be done at home. Ask students what jobs are done at home by more than one person. What jobs do you do? Do you have the same jobs at home as your classmates? Do you have the same jobs as your older or younger brothers and sisters? Why or why not? Have students look at the photographs and write answers to the questions. **For the first photograph, students should respond that the mom, sister, and brother are helping. Students should tell how they help at home. Answers will vary.**

Page 16
Explain that there are many ways for families to have fun. Ask students to name ways families have fun together at home. (playing games and sports, cooking together, reading, watching television, telling stories) Ask students if they have fun when they go places. Invite them to tell about places they have gone with their families where they had fun. Ask students to explain who or what made the experience fun. Call students' attention to the photographs. **Students should put a checkmark on the family at home in the bottom photograph. They should draw a line under the families on the Ferris wheel and the family at the science center.**

Page 17
Ask students why we have rules. Guide them to understand that rules help keep us safe and help people live and work together. Ask students to name some rules at school. Discuss some of the rules and help students understand how the rules keep them safe and help them live together at school. Invite students to share some clean-up rules and safety rules they must follow at home. Write the words *clean-up rules* and *safety rules* on the board and list the rules students name. Ask students if everyone has the same rules. **Students should write *safety rule* below the photograph on the left of an adult teaching a child a safety rule. They should write *clean-up rule* below the photograph at the right of children learning a clean-up rule at home.**

Project Tip
Read the Project Tip with students and discuss what students are to do. You may want to suggest that, after talking to their families, students should write down the rules or draw pictures to show the rules.

Page 18

Discuss the photographs with students. Point out that a child is saying good-night to his parents in one photo and three children are washing up before bed in the other photograph. Tell students that these are bedtime rules in these homes. Ask students why families have bedtime rules. Emphasize that some rules—like going to bed at a good hour, taking a bath, and brushing teeth—are rules that keep children healthy. Ask students to tell some of their bedtime rules. Make a list on the board and then ask students how family rules are alike and how they are different. **Students should put a checkmark next to the following rules: Go to bed at a good hour; Put your toys away; Brush your teeth.** Discuss the other answer choice, helping students to understand why it is not a rule.

Page 19

Around the Globe Discuss the photographs with children. Point out to students that the photographs are pictures of families working and playing together in other countries. Invite students to tell what is happening in each photograph. Then ask students to compare the things their families do with what the families in the photographs are doing. Lead students to understand that families in other countries are both similar to and different from United States families. Discuss the title of the feature, "Families Together," with students. Ask students why this is a good title for this feature. **Students should circle the picture of the father and son at the lower left. They should draw a line under the photograph of the street festival.**

Page 20

Chapter Checkup You may want to work through the Chapter Checkup with students. Make sure they all understand what the correct answers are.

Answers: Students should put a checkmark under the picture of the family having a picnic. They should draw a line under the picture of a mother and daughter at a traffic signal.

Encourage several students to volunteer their ideas about why we need rules. Many will respond that we need rules to keep us safe as well as to help us live and work together.

After Reading the Chapter

Have students form several small groups. Ask each group to pretend they are a family. Have them role-play a situation in which the family plans a trip to a ball game or the circus.

Social Studies
If students know a family from another country, ask them to think of a way the family is different than their own family. Have them draw a picture or tell a story that shows one difference. Examples might include a special holiday tradition, a special food, or a style of clothing. Have them tell how the family is like their own family, too.

Writing
Have students write a description of one evening at home with their family. Tell them to write about ways the family has fun together.

Art
Have students draw pictures that show how they and their families work together. Tell students to focus on one activity only, such as cleaning up after dinner. Students may want to write the names of their family members on their pictures.

Writing
Ask students to write three rules they have in their family. Have them tell which is the best rule, and why.

Social Studies
Point out to students that even when people are having fun or playing they still need to obey rules. Have small groups of students think of some rules that need to be followed for the following recreational activities: kickball, swimming, and watching a movie. Ask groups to tell about some of the rules for these activities.

Unit Summary All families have basic needs for food, clothing, and shelter. Economics and geography help determine our needs and how we meet them. Families also have wants. Each family chooses how best to meet its needs and wants.

Before Reading the Unit Show students pictures of things such as a doll, milk, ice cream, an apple, and a house. Include both needs and wants. Ask students: Which of these things do you need the most in order to live? What would happen if you did not have ice cream? Milk? A house?

Then have the students read the unit opener on page 23 and look at the picture. Ask students what needs and wants they see in the photograph. Call students' attention to the questions on the page and tell students to keep them in mind as they read this unit.

Point out the Unit Project box, and tell students they will work on this project during the unit.

Unit Project

Setting Up the Project Collect a variety of magazines that include pictures of needs and wants for students to cut out. Tell students they will be collecting and making many pictures. Help students find ways to keep materials together until the project is completed.

Students will find specific suggestions in the Project Tip sections of the chapters. Encourage them to adapt the suggestions to their own interests.

Presenting the Project One alternate possibility is that students might separate the pictures into needs, wants, and jobs. They could then create three collages by pasting the pictures on poster board. They could cut out the items to make interesting shapes.

After Reading the Unit Ask students to discuss the unit opener questions. Prompt discussion by asking additional questions. Can things we want also be things we need? How do people earn money to buy needs and wants? Why must people make choices about needs and wants? What are some of your needs and wants?

Skill Builder

Making a List

Before students read page 44, explain that a list is a helpful way to organize and to remember information. Ask volunteers to tell about some of the kinds of lists people make. Explain that they will be organizing needs and wants by making lists.

Answers: Under "Needs", students should list: home, clothing; students should draw a third need and write it on the line. Under "Wants", students should list: toys, pets; students should draw a third want and write the name of the want on the line.

Bibliography

Teacher

Ellis, A. K. *Teaching and Learning Elementary Social Studies.* 4th edition, Allyn & Bacon, 1991.

Geography for Life: National Geography Standards, 1994. NCGE.

Hoven-Severson, L. *Connecting Geography to Literature.* Teacher Created Materials, Inc., 1992.

Natoli, S. (ed.). *Strengthening Geography in the Social Studies.* National Council for the Social Studies, 1992.

Rice, Melanie and Chris. *All About Things People Do.* Doubleday, 1990.

Student

Carlson, Judy. *Life with Max.* (Real Reading Series) Steck-Vaughn, 1989. (Grades 0–2)

Goldish, Meish. *The Same But Different.* (Real Reading Series) Steck-Vaughn, 1989. (Grades 1–2)

Miller, Marilyn. *The Airport.* (Behind the Scenes Series) Steck-Vaughn, 1989. (Grades 2–3)

Miller, Marilyn. *The Shopping Mall.* (Behind the Scenes Series) Steck-Vaughn, 1989. (Grades 2–3)

Teacher's Resource Binder

Blackline Masters for Unit 2: Unit 2 Project Organizer, Unit 2 Review, Unit 2 Test; Activities for Chapters 3, 4, 5

Chapter Summary Families have basic needs and wants. A need is something a person must have to live, and a want is something a person would like to have. Families need food, which they may buy or grow. Families also need homes, of which there are many kinds, and clothing, which they buy or make. Families want many kinds of things. Some of these things can be either needs or wants.

Chapter Objectives Students will learn to

• identify food, clothing, and shelter as basic family needs.

• tell the ways in which homes protect us.

• identify ways in which families supply food and clothing.

• distinguish between needs and wants.

Vocabulary

need, p. 24   want, p. 24

Vocabulary Activities On chart paper or on the chalkboard, write the following two sentences: *I need a dog. I need a home.* Underline *need.* After reading both sentences with students, discuss which item is more important. Tell students that a need is something that keeps us alive. Explain that a want is something we would like to have but don't need to have in order to live. Show students who have difficulty with the vocabulary terms how to use the glossary.

Before Reading the Chapter Display a group of pictures that show different kinds of homes. Ask students to identify the different kinds of homes. Ask who might live in the various homes. Next, hold an apple in one hand and a lollipop in the other. Allow students to decide which item is something they need and which is something they may want. Discuss students' reasons for their answers.

Teaching Suggestions and Answers
Page 24
Before students read the page, make two lists on the chalkboard, one labeled "Needs" and one labeled "Wants." Ask students to name things they need and want. Write items on the list that students indicate. Then have students read the page. Discuss needs and wants. Then, look again at the lists with students and evaluate each item to see if students still think it is in the correct column. Have students look at the pictures. **They should draw circles around the plate of food, shirt, and jacket; they should put checkmarks on the baseball bat, teddy bear, and ice cream cone.**

Page 25
Ask students what would happen if we did not have food. (We would get sick, weak, and starve.) Point out that food is one of our basic needs. Ask students where their families get food. Encourage students to tell about any foods they grow at home. Ask them to tell who prepares the food they eat. Do they help? How? You might then explain that certain kinds of foods provide nutrition that the body requires to remain healthy and strong. Emphasize that we need these foods. Other foods do not provide good nutrition. Point out that we often eat these foods because we like them, but they are not foods we need. Have students name kinds of foods we need and kinds of foods we want. **Students should draw a line to match the picture of the person growing food with the sentence, "We grow food." They should draw another line to match the picture of the person buying food with the sentence, "We buy food."**

Page 26
Discuss different types of homes with students. Ask students why we need a home. Lead them to understand that a home gives us a place to sleep, to keep warm and dry, and to stay safe. Have students look at the photographs. Ask them how these homes are alike. (All provide people with shelter.) How are they different? (Answers will vary.) **Students should circle the photograph of the apartment building. They should underline the photograph of the mobile homes.**

Page 27
Ask students what would happen if we did not have warm clothing on a winter day or cool clothing for a hot summer day. Discuss the need

for different kinds of clothing for different weather and seasons. Discuss the difference between "fun" clothing, like costumes and party clothes, and "necessary" clothes like shirts and gloves. Have students look at the photographs and tell what is happening in each one. **Students should circle the top left picture of the person buying clothes.**

Page 28

Ask students to name some things they want but do not need in order to live. Then ask students to think about activities they want to do and activities they need to do. Is going to the movies a want or a need? Is going to school a want or a need? Help students make these distinctions. Have students look at the photographs and describe what they see. **Students should circle the picture of the girl on the horse. Students should draw a line under the picture of the boys at the campsite.**

Project Tip

Read the tip with students and discuss what they should do. Explain that they can draw pictures of things or activities.

Page 29

Discuss with students whether all people have all the things they need. Invite students to suggest ways that we can help people who do not have all they need. Possible answers include donating food and clothing and donating money to provide shelter. **Students should list specific things they need and want. Items listed as needs should include food, clothing, and a place to live. Items listed as wants will vary, but might include toys, pets, video games, or movie tickets.**

Page 30

Around the Globe Tell students to look at the photographs and the title of the feature. Explain that people in other countries may have different ways of eating. Tell students that the children eating with chopsticks live in China. The family that is eating with their hands lives in Saudi Arabia. **Students should put an X on the picture of the family eating with their hands. They should draw a line over the family eating with chopsticks. They should circle the people who are shopping for food.**

Page 31

Chapter Checkup You may want to work through the Chapter Checkup with students. Make sure they all understand what the correct answers are.

Answers: Students should write an *N* on the house, socks, and milk in the top row. Students should circle the house and house trailer below the top row.

Ask students to share their answers. They should recognize that a bike is a want because you do not need a bike to live.

After Reading the Chapter

Have students draw pictures of different kinds of shelters they have seen in their neighborhood or town.

Art

Have students choose one thing people need and create a poster that shows and tells why it is needed.

Writing

Have students think of two clothing items they need in the winter and two items they need in the summer. Then have them write an explanation of why these things are needs and not wants.

Health

Have students create two columns on chart paper. They should title the columns "Foods We Need" and "Foods We Want." Have them cut pictures of food out of magazines and paste them in the appropriate columns.

Chapter Summary Families work in order to earn money to buy things they need and want. Some people work at home; others work away from home at stores, offices, and factories. Some workers help keep people safe; others help them learn. Children can work, too.

Chapter Objectives Students will learn to

- identify some ways in which people earn money.

- understand that people work to buy the things they need and want.

- name the kinds of jobs that children can do to help at home and to earn money.

Vocabulary Activities There are no new vocabulary words for this chapter. Since the focus of the chapter is on work, however, it would be a good idea to review the word *work*.

Make a word web using the word *work*. You may want to use the Concept Web graphic organizer found on page 48 of this guide for this activity. Write *work* at the center of the web and ask students to think of as many different kinds of work as they can. Encourage them to think of work that children do as well as work that adults do. Ask questions so that students can talk about work in many different ways. For example: What kind of work do some of the adults you know do? Students' responses should include the word *work*. For example, "My aunt works at a store." "My neighbor works at an insurance company." Underline the word *work* in each response.

Before Reading the Chapter Show students pairs of pictures. In each pair of pictures, one picture should show a person earning money, and the other picture should show a person playing or relaxing. For example, one picture might show an adult working in a supermarket; the other might show an adult reading a newspaper. Have students select the person who is at work and identify the job that is being done. Ask students to tell what they think the person might do with the money he or she earns. Show students other pictures, such as a boy or girl walking a dog or setting a table. Have students think of jobs a child might do to earn money. Ask students to tell how they think a child might use the money he or she earns.

Teaching Suggestions and Answers
Page 32
Ask students to tell who works in their family. Discuss why people work, emphasizing that people need to earn money so they can buy the things they need and want. Direct students' attention to the two photographs. **Students should put a checkmark on the photograph of the farmer and draw a line under the photograph of the baby-sitter.** Ask students: Do any members of your family baby-sit or work on a farm? If they do, ask students to tell about the work. Then ask what other jobs could be done at home to earn money. (baking, sewing, word processing, painting and other forms of art, fixing cars)

Page 33
Ask students what people who work in a store do. (sell things, stock shelves, help customers) Ask students what people who work in a factory do. (make things) Then discuss what happens to the goods made in a factory. Help students see that the products go to stores where they are sold. Ask students to look at the photograph. **Students should circle *factory* and *They make things*. Invite students to name some other places where people work.**

Project Tip
Discuss the Project Tip with students and help them see how this activity relates to the chapter topic. When students finish their pictures, have them tell members of their team about their pictures.

Page 34
Explain to students that some people work to make and sell us the things we need and want. Other people work to help us. Explain that some of these people work to keep us safe. Ask students to name people who have these jobs. (firefighters, police officers, school crossing guards, ambulance drivers) Then tell students that some people work to help us learn. Have students name some of these workers. (teachers, librarians, scout masters, sports coaches) Direct students' attention to the photographs, and have students identify the worker in each. **Students**

should then circle the photographs of the teacher and the librarian. They should draw a line under the photograph of the firefighters.

Page 35

Discuss the kinds of jobs that children do at home, such as making beds, taking out trash, setting the table, and feeding and walking the dog. Invite students to tell what kinds of jobs they do at home. Then discuss the kinds of jobs children might do to earn money. Have students look at the photographs and tell what these children are doing to earn money. (shoveling snow, raking leaves) Ask students to name other jobs children can do, such as running errands and doing yard work. Ask students what children might do with the money they earn. **Students should write the name of some kind of work they would like to do. Answers will vary.**

Page 36

Special People Ask volunteers to tell about the various places a nurse has helped them. These might include the hospital, school, and doctor's office. Ask: What jobs does a nurse do? (give shots, take temperatures, bandage cuts) You might tell students that Clara Barton was known as the "Angel of the Battlefield" because of her work on the battlefields during the Civil War. She later established the American Red Cross after learning about the work of the International Red Cross in Europe. Today the American Red Cross provides many services during wars and natural disasters, including giving food, clothing, and shelter to people in need. **Students should draw a picture of a nurse. Students' drawings will vary.**

Page 37

Chapter Checkup You may want to work through the Chapter Checkup with students. Make sure students understand what the correct answers are to the numbered questions.

Answers: Students should write *1* next to the picture of the girl carrying out the trash; they should write *2* next to the picture of the man teaching a boy to swim.

Let several students volunteer their ideas about the workers named. Possible answers include doctors, nurses, dentists, teachers, parents.

After Reading the Chapter

Ask students to look for a worker on their way to school each day and to observe what the worker does. Tell them to give their classmates clues about the worker. Have classmates guess what the worker's job is. Help students make a list of all the different kinds of workers they identify.

Social Studies

Make arrangements to visit one or more public buildings, such as the fire station, post office, library, or police station. Have students make pictures of the workers and write a sentence telling one task that each worker does in his or her job.

Writing

Have students talk to an adult about a job he or she does. Have them write a description of what the person does at the job.

Art

Ask students to draw a picture showing what kind of job they would like to do when they grow up. Tell students to write a sentence at the bottom of their picture that tells what they would do at the job.

Chapter Summary Families must make choices. Families must choose the kind of home they will have, and if they need a car, the kind of car they drive. In addition to making choices that meet needs, families make choices about things they want. Because they cannot afford everything, they have to choose the things they want most.

Chapter Objectives Students will learn to

- discuss the reasons families make the choices they do in selecting homes, food, clothing, and entertainment.

- explain how choices are made because of family economics, needs, and wants.

Vocabulary Activities Discuss the word *choose*. Explain that some things are very hard to choose. Show students pictures of five popular games or foods. Tell students that they can choose only one of the items. Is it hard to choose? Why? (It is hard to choose if you want more than one thing. It is not hard to choose if you know exactly what you want.)

Before Reading the Chapter Set up a "play" store using items in the classroom or children's toys as the items to be sold. Give students play money with which to purchase the items. As each student makes a purchase, ask why that item was chosen. Ask students to think about why they want the item and whether they have enough money to buy it. You can designate a price that is more than the student has so that the student may have to make another choice.

Teaching Suggestions and Answers
Page 38
Ask students if they have ever had to make a choice among several toys. Encourage them to tell how they made the choice by examining the toys, thinking about how they would play with each one, and deciding on the one they most wanted. Prompt additional discussion by asking: Can you spend as much money as you want on a toy? Do you have space in your room for a huge toy? Explain that families also must make choices about the things they buy. They must decide what they can afford, what they need, what they will use most, whether they have space for the item, and so on.

Tell students to look at the picture. Ask them to tell what is happening in the picture. **In responding to the question, most students will explain that it is a good place for a family because it has a lot of room for a family and a yard for children to play in.**

Page 39
Begin a discussion with students about different kinds of homes: apartment houses, single-family houses, two- and three-family houses, mobile homes, and so on. Explain that in many cases, the kind of home people can choose is determined by the place where they live. Large, multi-story apartment blocks are often found in large cities, small apartment complexes in suburbs, single-family houses mostly in suburbs and smaller towns, and so on. In the city, many families need a place to live. Because there is not a lot of space, people construct tall buildings with many apartments for a number of individuals and families. In the suburbs and smaller towns, there is more space. Direct students' attention to the pictures on pages 38 and 39. Ask them which home they would probably find in a city. Discuss students' answers. **Students should respond to the picture on page 39 by circling the answer *many families*.**

Page 40
Discuss how families choose cars. Explain that a family may consider many factors, such as cost, the size of the family, whether the car will be used for driving to work or for family trips. Point out that many families who live in large cities do not own cars. People use public transportation such as buses and subway and commuter trains to get from place to place. Explain that heavy traffic, traffic jams, and expensive parking can be problems in cities. Then ask students to name some advantages of public transportation. (people don't have to deal with traffic, people don't have to look for parking or pay for it) Tell students to look at the cars on this page and think about the family pictured that must make a choice. **Students should circle the car they think the family should choose. Answers will vary. Accept all reasonable explanations for answers.**

Project Tip
Discuss the tip with students. Suggest they think about different types of homes in their neighborhood or in neighborhoods they have visited.

Page 41
Discuss how the amount of money a family has affects their choices. Tell students that in this picture, the father is going to make only one purchase, either the bike or the shoes. Ask students which choice he should make, and why. Guide students to understand that he should probably choose the shoes because shoes are a need, but a bicycle is a want. **Answers to the question will vary. Possible response: People don't have enough money to buy everything they want.**

Page 42
Did You Know? Tell students that many groups make choices by voting. Ask students how else a group might make a choice. (One person might choose for everyone.) Discuss why voting is a good way to make choices, leading students to appreciate that everyone gets to have input. Be sure students understand that voting does not guarantee that your choice will win, but does guarantee that a majority of the people who voted will get their choice. **Students should write about a situation in which they voted. Answers will vary.**

Page 43
Chapter Checkup You may want to work through the Chapter Checkup with students to make sure students understand the correct answers.

Answers: Students should circle the picture of the house; they should put an X on the turkey. Ask several students to share their responses. Possible answer: They do not have enough money to buy everything.

After Reading the Chapter
Provide students with some practice in distinguishing between needs and wants. Make some large flashcards with the following words: *House, Cat, Shirt, Milk, Skates, Air, Bike, TV,* and *Cake.* Flash each of the cards and have volunteers call out whether the card represents a need or a want.

Writing
Have each student draw a picture of something he or she really wants but has been told is too expensive. Then ask students to think of ways they might get the too-expensive item at a later time. Have them write a plan for getting the item.

Social Studies
Have students each draw two pictures. One picture should be of a need and the other picture should be of a want. Ask students to trade their pictures with another classmate. Students should identify their partners' pictures by writing *need* or *want* on the pictures.

Drama
Organize the class into different-sized groups ranging from two persons to eight. Tell students to imagine they are families who are looking for a new home. Encourage students to take on the roles of different family members and work together to make a choice on the size and location of their new home. Have groups tell the rest of the class how they made their choices and what different factors influenced their decision making.

Unit Summary School is a place where people learn, play, and make friends. Rules help people live and work together harmoniously and safely, in school and in the neighborhood.

Before Reading the Unit Take students for a walk around the school neighborhood. When you return, ask them questions about what they saw. How many buildings are places where people live? How many are places to work? Where do people play? How do people get to places where they work?

Extend the discussion to find out what students would like to know about the neighborhood. Have them read the unit opener on page 46 and discuss the photograph. Why do students think the photograph shows a neighborhood? Ask students to read the questions. Tell them they will learn the answers to these questions as they work on this unit.

Ask students to look at the Unit Project box. Discuss the directions with students.

Unit Project

Setting Up the Project Create opportunities for students to learn about the school neighborhood. Encourage class discussion of the things people do in the neighborhood. You might want to lead students on visits to specific places. If practical, allow students to talk to people who work in the neighborhood.

Students will find specific suggestions in the Project Tip sections of the chapters. Encourage them to adapt the suggestions to their own interests.

Presenting the Project Students can follow the suggestions on page 67 or choose other ways to present their projects. One alternative possibility is to create a picture map of the neighborhood on chart paper. Students might model it on the one on pages 58–59. They can paste their pictures on the map in places where the buildings belong. The team can give a "tour" of the neighborhood by orally walking the class through their map.

After Reading the Unit Invite discussion of the questions on the unit opener. Prompt further discussion by asking more questions. What is your favorite place in the neighborhood? Why?

Do many people live in the neighborhood? What kind of work do people do in the neighborhood?

Skill Builder
Using a Map Key
As students read page 66, remind them that a map key tells what the pictures on the map represent. Review the concept by pointing out a building on the map and then having students find a building that looks just like that picture in the map key. Emphasize that it is the same picture and that the key tells what it is.

Answers: 1. Students should color a sidewalk red. **2.** Students should put a blue *X* on the store. **3.** 4 houses

Bibliography
Teacher
Disinger, J. F. *Environment in the K–12 Curriculum: An Overview.* Milwood Kraus International, 1993.
Fromboluti, C. *Helping Your Child Learn Geography.* U.S. Department of Education, 1990.
Huff, Barbara A. *Greening the City Streets: The Story of Community Gardens.* Clarion Books, 1990.
Rice, Melanie and Chris. *All About Things People Do.* Doubleday, 1990.
Winston, Barbara J. *Map and Globe Skills: K–8 Teaching Guide.* NCGE, 1986.

Student
Bailey, Donna. *Farmers.* (Facts About Series) Steck-Vaughn, 1990. (Grades 2–3)
Birnbaum, Bette. *My School, Your School.* (Ready • Set • Read Series) Steck-Vaughn, 1992. (Grade 1)
Humphrey, Paul. *Let's Work Together.* (Read All About It Series) Steck-Vaughn, 1995. (Grade 2)
Ramsay, Helena, and Paul Humphrey. *Wheels, Wheels, Wheels.* (Read All About It Series) Steck-Vaughn, 1995. (Grade 2)

Teacher's Resource Binder

Blackline Masters for Unit 3: Unit 3 Project Organizer, Unit 3 Review, Unit 3 Test; Activities for Chapters 6, 7

Chapter Summary School is a place to work and play. Rules in school tell us what to do and what not to do. Schools have playgrounds. Teachers and librarians help us learn in school.

Chapter Objectives Students will learn to

- identify the functions of a school.

- demonstrate the meaning of direction terms.

- discuss the meaning of and reasons for rules.

- read a picture graph.

- name the people who work in a school building.

Vocabulary

picture graph, p. 52

Vocabulary Activities Although *rules* was introduced in Chapter 2, it will be reviewed here. Write the following words on flashcards: *rules, picture graph*. Read the words to students as you show them the cards. Then read aloud these riddles: I help you know what to do or what not to do. What am I? (rules) I help you count things. I show how many. What am I? (picture graph) Have students guess the answers and identify the correct flashcard.

Before Reading the Chapter Provide time for students to share what they know about school. On the chalkboard or on chart paper, write each student's contribution. Tell students that as they read, they may add more information to the charts. Play a familiar game. Then play the game without following the rules. Ask which way is better, and why.

Teaching Suggestions and Answers
Page 47
Explain to students that all communities have schools. Ask students what kinds of things they learn in school. Ask them to look at the photographs and to tell what the students are doing. Then ask how many children are working together in the building-block photograph. Guide students to understand that working together is an

important school activity. By learning to work together, children learn to share, take turns, plan, and clean up when finished. **Students should circle the following sentences:** *I play with friends. I learn to read and write. I learn to share. I work with my teacher.*

Page 48
Explain to students that this picture shows a classroom as seen from up above the room. Guide students in identifying the teacher, flagpole, student desks, windows, door, chalkboard, rabbits, plant, and so on. Then help students practice understanding relative location. First ask them to stand and face in one direction. Ask them to point to the *right* side of the room and then to the *left* side. Have students locate things on the *right* and *left* sides of your classroom. Use words such as *behind, on top of, in front of, next to,* and *under* while having them locate things in the classroom. Then direct their attention back to the picture. Ask questions such as: What is behind the teacher's desk? (a chair, the chalkboard) What is next to the flagpole? (a bookcase, the teacher) What is to the left of the plant? (a table) **Students should circle** *rabbit* **and** *window.*

Page 49
Tell students to look at the picture on this page. Explain that it is a drawing of the classroom on page 48. Ask them how it is the same as the first picture. (Both have desks, windows, bookcases, doors, and so on.) Ask them how this drawing is different. (There are no people, animals, books, and so on.) Point out that the bookcase, desks, chalkboard, and other things in this drawing are in the same position as they are in the first picture. **Answers to the first question will vary, but may include: the chair, chalkboard, flag, wastebasket, door. Answers to the second question may also vary but might include the chalkboard, bookcase, wastebasket, teacher's desk.**

Page 50
Ask students to identify some rules they have in school. Ask students to name other places where they have rules. (home, community, playground)

Now have students look at the photographs, and ask them to tell what is happening in each. Ask them to think of some rules that would be helpful in each situation. **Students should write a _1_ above the classroom photograph and _2_ above the playground photograph.**

Project Tip

Suggest that each team member draw a different part of your school (*e.g.,* the library, gym, cafeteria, or art room). Encourage students also to show in their drawings what people do in different parts of the school.

Page 51

Discuss some of the rules students have identified, and explain how the rules help keep people safe, keep things fair, and help people live together. Discuss the picture with students. Ask: What could the boy do to follow the rule? **They should respond to the first question by writing _Do not litter._ Students should write a rule that they feel helps them the most. Answers will vary.**

Page 52

Explain that a picture graph arranges facts and numbers in ways that are easy to understand. Tell them that this picture graph shows how many slides and trees are in the playground that is pictured. Have them count the trees in the picture and the trees in the picture graph. Then have them count the slides in each. Help them understand that the picture graph is a way of arranging information taken from the picture. Point out that one column on the picture graph is labeled for slides and one for trees. The rows that show how many are numbered. **Students should respond to the first question by writing _5_ and to the second by writing _3_.** Ask students to tell about their playground. How many swings are there? How many slides? Do you have other things in your playground? Have them direct you in creating a picture graph on the chalkboard for the playground equipment.

Page 53

Ask students to identify the adults who work in the school and to tell what they do. Discuss the pictures. Have students tell how each of these people helps them. Point out the words *librarian* and *teacher* in the text. **In response to the first question, students should write _librarian_ and in**

response to the second question, they should write *teacher.*

Page 54

Around the Globe If any students are from other countries, encourage them to tell about school in those countries. Have them compare schools there with their school here. Ask students to look at the photograph and tell ways the school is similar to and different from their own school. Ask students to name how all schools are the same. Guide students to understand that all schools have teachers and that students work, play, learn, and share in schools. Have them draw a picture of their school. **Drawings will vary.**

Page 55

Chapter Checkup Make sure all students understand what the correct answers are to the numbered questions.

Answers: 1. Students should draw a line under the illustration of the teacher. **2.** They should circle the rabbit. **3.** They should put an *X* on the chalkboard or on the teacher's chair. Ask several students to share their ideas. Answers will vary, but students should demonstrate an understanding that the class needs rules so that everyone can work, play, and learn together.

After Reading the Chapter

Make a list of classroom rules, such as speaking rules or clean-up rules. Have students choose a rule and draw two pictures, one showing what would happen if students did not follow the rule and one showing what happens when students follow the rule.

Social Studies

Guide students on a tour of the school. Have students talk to school workers and learn what the workers do. Have students write what they know about one worker's job.

Writing

Write this sentence on the chalkboard: I'd like to be a _____ . Have students copy the sentence and fill in the blank with the name of a kind of school worker. Then have them write two or three more sentences telling why.

Chapter Summary A neighborhood is a place where families live, work, and play. There are many kinds of neighborhoods, but all are alike in some ways. There are also many kinds of places in a neighborhood. Neighborhoods change over time.

Chapter Objectives Students will learn to

- describe the characteristics of a neighborhood.

- read a picture map.

- find places on a map using a map key.

- identify cardinal directions.

- name ways in which neighborhoods change.

Vocabulary

neighborhood, p. 56	map key, p. 60
map, p. 60	directions, p. 61

Vocabulary Activities Introduce the words *neighborhood, map, map key,* and *directions* in a class discussion. Write each word on a flashcard. Hold up each flashcard and read the word aloud. Ask if anyone can tell what the word means. Model using each word in a sentence. Follow this procedure with the other new words. Remind students who have trouble with vocabulary terms that they can use the glossary to find the meanings of the words.

Before Reading the Chapter Show students a variety of maps. Explain that maps help us find the way to places. Ask students how a map can help a bus driver or a mail carrier. Have a student give directions to various rooms in the school. Ask students what might make direction-giving easier. Guide them to understand that a picture, or a map, is helpful.

Teaching Suggestions and Answers
Page 56

Discuss the definition of a neighborhood with students. Give examples of places in the school neighborhood where people live, work, and play. Ask students to look at the photographs.

Have them tell about similar places in their neighborhoods. Ask students to describe some of the buildings and places where they play. **Students should put a checkmark next to the top left picture of the neighborhood. They should put an X next to the picture of the place to work at the bottom of the page. They should draw a line over the picture of the place to play in the top right photograph.**

Page 57

Ask students to tell about the neighborhoods they have lived in or visited. Encourage students to tell how the neighborhoods were different and how they were similar to the neighborhood they live in now. Tell students to look at the photographs and tell which neighborhood is most like theirs. **Students should respond that both neighborhoods are places where families live, work, and play.**

Pages 58 and 59

Look at the map that covers pages 58 and 59. Take students on a tour of the neighborhood pictured, starting at Ann's house. Follow the road and read the labels on each building. Have children point to each building with their fingers as you say its name. **Students should circle Green Park; they should draw a line under the picture of the supermarket; and, they should put a checkmark next to the apartment building.**

Have students find places on the map where people work. (bank, school, fire station, supermarket, post office, the location of the road work) Give students additional practice with relative location. Ask them questions such as: Whose house is *next to* Anita's house? Which building is *behind* the school? What building is *near* the post office?

Page 60

Have students look at the map that covers pages 60 and 61. Have students put their finger on the map key. Discuss the map key with students, explaining that each picture in the key stands for a kind of building, not a particular building. The house, for example, is any house. Have students find corresponding pictures on the map on pages 60 and 61. **Students should put a check mark under the house. They should draw a line under the school.**

Be sure that students understand that this is a map of the same neighborhood they looked at on pages 58 and 59. Help them turn back to pages 58 and 59 and find corresponding places on the picture. For example, have them find and compare Paul's house in the picture and on the map. Discuss how the map shows the same places as the picture, but the drawings on the map are much simpler.

Page 61

Have students point out each of the direction arrows on the map and read the directions—north, south, east, west—as they do so. **Students should draw a line under the school. They should circle *Green Park* on page 60.**

Page 62

Ask students if their family has ever moved from one house to another. Invite them to tell how the new home was different from the old one. Ask if their family changed the way the home looked after they moved in. How? Discuss ways that families can change their homes on the outside by painting, repairing, planting flowers, and so on. Discuss how changes to a home are also changes to a neighborhood. Ask students to describe some changes they have observed in their neighborhood. Encourage them to think about new building construction, street repairs, and other changes. Have students look at the photographs. **They should put a red checkmark next to the top picture of the family moving. They should draw a line under the picture on the left of the family planting a garden.**

Project Tip
Read the tip aloud. Suggest students look for places people work as they go to and from school and on errands with their parents. Encourage them to ask questions about these places and to learn what people do in their jobs at these places.

Page 63

Special People Explain to students that when Benjamin Franklin lived (1706–1790), there were no cars, jets, or televisions. Where Franklin lived—in Philadelphia, Pennsylvania—there were no hospitals and no public libraries. Franklin started a public library and the first city hospital in America. Talk with students about their school library. Help them identify the kinds of things they have in the library, such as the librarian's desk, bookcases, reading tables, and so on. You might want to write some of these items on the chalkboard as reminders for students as they draw their library maps. **Maps should depict the school library and should include a map key.**

Page 64

Did You Know? Discuss any historic homes or other buildings in your community. If you know the history of these buildings, share it with students. Explain that these buildings help us know what life was like long ago. Have students look at the photograph of the log cabin. Discuss with them how it is similar to and different from homes of today. **Students should write a question they would like to ask someone who lived in the cabin. Questions will vary.**

Page 65

Chapter Checkup You may want to work through the Chapter Checkup with students.

Answers: Students should write *map* next to the first illustration, *map key* next to the second illustration, and *neighborhood* next to the third illustration. Ask students to share their answers. Possible answers include: people move in and out; houses are built or remodeled; trees and flowers are planted.

After Reading the Chapter

Have students work together to make a map of the classroom. Using large mural paper, have students draw picture symbols for the desks, closets, windows, doors, etc. Students could write their names on the desks. Have students draw arrows for each of the cardinal directions.

Writing
Have students think about a change they would like to make in their neighborhood. Have them write a description of what they would do.

Unit Summary We live on planet Earth, which is a sphere. A globe is a model of Earth. Earth is composed of many landforms, including mountains and rivers. Earth provides the resources families need and want. Pollution destroys our resources, but people can stop pollution and clean up Earth.

Before Reading the Unit Display pictures of various landforms and physical features, such as mountains, plains, seashores, and deserts. Explain that all these places are part of the planet we share. Show students a relief map or globe so that they can understand the variety of land surfaces on Earth.

Have students read the unit opener and look at the photograph. Ask them to tell how they would feel if they visited the place shown. Have students look at the questions. Tell them to look for answers as they read this unit.

Point out the Unit Project box. Explain that this is the project they will work on as they read this unit.

Unit Project

Setting Up the Project You might want to brainstorm different kinds of places with your class in order to provide them with a variety of choices. Monitor choices to ensure that different kinds of landforms are represented.

Students will find specific suggestions in the Project Tip sections of the chapters. Encourage them to adapt the suggestions to their own interests.

Presenting the Project Students can follow the suggestions on page 85 or think of other ways to present their projects. One alternative might be for students to make a team oral presentation about their place. For example, they might divide up characteristics of the place, such as plants, animals, natural resources, climate, and other features. They can show pictures to the class and give oral descriptions and explanations about each of the characteristics.

After Reading the Unit Ask students what else they would like to know about the land and water of Earth. Prompt more discussion by asking questions. What kinds of resources are used where you live? How does pollution affect resources? How is your place different from some other places on Earth?

Skill Builder

Using a United States Map

Explain to students that a map of the United States can give them much information about our country. Point out the directional arrows and review what they tell about cardinal directions.

Answers: 1. Students should circle the arrow pointing North. **2.** They should color the land in the continental U.S. as well as Hawaii and Alaska in the inset maps brown. **3.** They should color any one state in the South green. **4.** They should color all the water blue. **5.** They should draw a tree in the West.

Bibliography

Teacher
Geography for Life: National Geography Standards, 1994. NCGE.
Koch, M. *World Water Watch.* Greenwillow Books, 1993.
Paden, M. (ed.). *Teacher's Guide to World Resources.* World Resources Institute, 1994.
Posey-Pacak, Melissa L. *Earth at Risk.* NCGE, 1991.

Student
Amos, Janine. *Waste and Recycling.* (First Starts Series) Steck-Vaughn, 1993. (Grades 2–3)
Kallen, Stuart A. *If Trees Could Talk.* (Eco-Storybooks Series) Steck-Vaughn, 1993. (Grades 1–3)
Lakin, Patricia. *Trash and Treasure.* (My School Series) Steck-Vaughn, 1995. (Grades 2–3)
Nielsen, Shelly. *Love Earth: The Beauty Makeover.* (Eco-Storybooks Series) Steck-Vaughn, 1993. (Grades 1–3)
Nielsen, Shelly. *Trash! Trash! Trash!* (Eco-Storybooks Series) Steck-Vaughn, 1993. (Grades 1–3)

Teacher's Resource Binder

Blackline Masters for Unit 4: Unit 4 Project Organizer, Unit 4 Review, Unit 4 Test; Activities for Chapters 8, 9; Outline Maps of the United States and the World

Chapter Summary A globe is a model of planet Earth that shows land and water. Earth is very large, and has different kinds of places, such as mountains, flat land, rivers, and oceans. People live and work in many kinds of places.

Chapter Objectives Students will learn to

- identify that we live on Earth and that Earth is round like a ball.

- recognize that a globe is a model of Earth.

- identify some of the landforms found in the United States and other parts of the world.

Vocabulary	
Earth, p. 69	mountains, p. 71
globe, p. 70	rivers, p. 72

Vocabulary Activities Place a flashcard with the word *globe* next to your classroom globe. Find some pictures or photographs of rivers and mountains and display flashcards with the words *rivers* and *mountains* on the pictures or photographs. Have students form small groups. The groups should write a riddle about each of the new vocabulary words. For example: What is round and is home to all people? (Earth) Each group can then read their riddle to the other groups. Students can respond by holding up the appropriate flashcard.

Before Reading the Chapter Take a walk around the school area. Have students notice the landforms and bodies of water (hills, rivers, brooks, for example). Ask students to think of at least one way a family uses the land to get the things they need. (use the soil to grow food, cut trees to build homes)

Teaching Suggestions and Answers

Page 69

Have students look at the photograph. Explain that this photograph was taken by astronauts traveling in space far from Earth. Ask students: What is the difference between a photograph and a drawing? Explain that a photograph is a picture that is taken by a camera. A drawing is a picture made by a person. Explain that Earth is shaped like a ball. Show students a cube and a ball. Allow students to discuss differences in shape. Pass the ball around. Ask students how much of the ball they can see without turning it. Elicit that they can see only one half at a time. **Students should circle *no* as the answer**.

Page 70

Show students a globe. If possible, pass it around. Explain that a globe is a model of Earth; it is a ball that shows the land and water on Earth. Point out that the picture on this page is a drawing of a globe. Because the Earth is a ball, there are two pictures: one to show each side of the globe. Point out the United States. Explain that Alaska and Hawaii are part of the United States. You might also explain that Hawaii is made up of small islands that are too small to show up on this picture of the globe. **In responding to the questions, students should circle *blue*. They should draw a circle around the United States, including Alaska.**

Project Tip

Discuss the Project Tip with students. Encourage students to look closely at their pictures and to describe to one another the plants, animals, and people they see.

Page 71

Discuss the landforms in the area in which students live. Is the land hilly or flat? Are there mountains? Is there lots of water? Encourage students to tell about the landforms in other geographic areas they have visited. Have students look at the photographs. Point out that the picture of the cattle ranch shows both flat land and mountains. **Students should put a red checkmark next to the picture of the farm. They should put a green checkmark next to the mountains.**

Page 72

Create a word web on the chalkboard with *water* at the center. You may want to use the Concept Web graphic organizer found on page 48 of this guide for this purpose. Have students suggest words that name bodies of water. Possible responses: river, stream, creek, ocean, lake, pond. Tell students that this photograph shows the Mississippi River as it flows past the Gateway Arch in St. Louis, Missouri. Explain that the Mississippi River is one of the largest and longest rivers in the world. You might want to help students locate the Mississippi River on a map of the United States. Ask students to name any large bodies of water in their neighborhood or region. **Students should draw a picture of the area in which they live.**

Page 73

Ask volunteers to tell where their parents or other adults they know work. Ask if their parents live close by or far from their jobs. Tell students that people who live in certain kinds of areas often have jobs related to the place. For example, people who live near water sometimes have special jobs. Invite students to tell what some of these jobs might be. (fishing, boat repair, sailing, water safety, charter boat service) Invite students to tell what kinds of jobs people might have who live near mountains, forested land, or flat land. **Students should put a red checkmark next to the top picture of the men loading fish. They should put a blue checkmark next to the bottom picture of the woman working high above ground.**

Page 74

Around the Globe Remind students that Mexico is another country, and that the people there speak Spanish. Help them locate Mexico on a map of the world or one of North America. Point out that the man in the picture is doing a job suitable to the kind of place in which he lives. Ask students: Could this man earn a living by fishing or by teaching people how to ski in this place? Why? (No; he cannot be either of these things because he does not live near water or mountains.) **Students should circle one of the corn plants in the photograph. They should circle** *The farm is on flat land.*

Page 75

Did You Know? Have students look at the picture on page 75. Explain to them that this photograph is a computer-generated representation of how the proposed International Space Station, called Freedom, will look once it has been built. Mention to students that the space station is an international effort, with the United States, Europe, Canada, Japan, and Russia

expected to cooperate on the project. Help students understand the concept of outer space. You might tell students to look back at the picture of Earth on page 69, and explain that Earth is surrounded by space. Tell them there is no air in space, so astronauts who work there must wear special suits that supply them with air to breathe. **Students should write a question they would like to know about space.**

Page 76

Chapter Checkup You may want to work through the Chapter Checkup with students.

Answers: 1. round **2.** blue **3.** globe **4.** Answers will vary. Students should respond that the land in mountains is too steep to farm.

After Reading the Chapter

Have students create a bulletin-board display with three parts. Entitle it: "Things We Can Do on Mountains (Water, Flat Land)." Have students draw pictures or cut out photographs in magazines that show the activities of people living in the particular area. Students should display the pictures under the appropriate heading.

Art
Have students mold papier-mâché around a balloon to form a sphere. The sphere can be painted like a globe to show landforms and water.

Writing
Have students choose the kind of place where they would most like to live. Have them write an explanation of why they would like to live there.

Chapter Summary The natural resources of the United States include land, trees, air, and water. People cannot make some new resources, so we must take care of them. Sometimes, however, we allow pollution to spoil our resources. People can stop making pollution, and they can clean up dirty resources.

Chapter Objectives Students will learn to

- name some resources found in the United States.

- identify ways to help prevent pollution, thus fostering conservation.

Vocabulary

resources, p. 77   pollution, p. 80

Vocabulary Activities Tell students that anything that makes our air, land, or water dirty is called *pollution*. Explain that our air, land, and water are called *resources*. We need clean resources to stay alive. Write *resource* and *pollution* on flashcards. Have students identify pollution and resources by answering questions such as the following: What would you call air that is filled with lots of smoke from factories? (pollution) What would you call a river? (resource)

Before Reading the Chapter Ask students if they ever take empty cans and bottles to be recycled. Have students offer reasons why these items are recycled. Ask students to tell what happens to the cans and bottles. Have each student draw a picture of his or her bedroom when it is messy and a picture of it after it is cleaned. Discuss how each student feels about a dirty room and how he or she feels about a clean room.

Teaching Suggestions and Answers
Page 77
Discuss resources with students. Invite them to name resources they can see from the classroom window. Emphasize to students that people cannot make some new resources. Once certain resources are gone or used up, we no longer

have them. **Students should write *water* below the photograph of the stream and *trees* below the photograph of the forest.**

Page 78
Have students look at the map of the United States. Explain that this is a map of our country. The dotted lines show the borders of each of the states. Tell them the two inset maps show the states of Alaska and Hawaii, which are far from the other states. You might want to show students North America on a map or a globe and show them where Alaska and Hawaii are located. On the map, show students the state in which they live. **Students should write an *X* where they live.** Emphasize that this map, like others they have studied, has directions. Review the use of cardinal directions. Remind students that the letters *N, S, E,* and *W* stand for the directions north, south, east, and west.

Page 79
Students should write answers on the map on page 78. They should put a red checkmark in the West on the United States. They should put a blue checkmark in the South. They should put a green checkmark in the North. Explain to students that trees, rivers, and farmland are found in many places in the United States. Discuss any of these resources that are found in your region. To help students recognize the difference between resources and things that have been made by people, give students the following pairs of words and have them tell which of the two items is a resource: *apple tree* and *parking meter; lake* and *swimming pool; forest* and *supermarket*. Ask volunteers to explain why some of the items are resources and others are not.

Page 80
Explain that pollution can come from many sources. Factory smoke, car exhaust, and the plowing and burning of fields can cause air pollution. Soil and water can be polluted by agricultural use of fertilizers and herbicides, from the dumping of sewage into lakes and rivers, and from oil and chemical spills. Explain what can

happen to people and other living things when the environment is polluted. (Breathing becomes difficult, people become sick, there is no clean water to drink or farm with, the land itself can become unusable.) Explain that not all pollution is caused by factories, farms, and cities; some is caused by individuals who do not understand why pollution is bad. Discuss littering, throwing away cans, bottles, and newspapers that might be recycled, and so on. Have students look at the photographs. **They should put a red checkmark next to both photographs of clean resources in the second row, and a blue checkmark next to the photograph of the polluted resource at the top of the page.**

Page 81

Emphasize that pollution can be stopped, but that people must agree and work together to bring it about. Explain that students can help, too. Encourage students to talk about pollution they have observed and the things they can do to help. Guide them to thinking about specific things they can do, such as remembering not to litter and picking up litter in the schoolyard, neighborhood park, or on the sidewalks or roads in front of their homes. **Students should draw a sign in the box that tells people to stop polluting. Signs will vary.**

Project Tip
Call students' attention to the tip and discuss what they are to do. Tell them to think about how pollution can change the place they have chosen for their team project.

Page 82

Special People Theodore Roosevelt was President of the United States from 1901 to 1909. He was an early advocate of conservation. Although some of his practices would no longer be considered environmentally sound, some of his achievements continue to provide a foundation for current conservation efforts. Some of Roosevelt's achievements, in addition to establishing national parks, include the establishment of the National Forest Service, the addition of millions of acres to our national forests, and the promotion of efforts to preserve wildlife. **Students should write ideas about action they can take to protect our natural resources. Answers will vary.**

Page 83

Chapter Checkup You may want to work through the Chapter Checkup with students to make sure they understand what the correct answers are.

Answers: Students should write *water* under the picture of the children playing in the water. They should write *land* under the picture of the garden. Invite students to volunteer their ideas about pollution. Possible responses: pollution hurts everyone; pollution can make people sick.

After Reading the Chapter

Have students make "Clean-Up" buttons to wear around the school. Challenge students to create mottoes for their buttons, such as "Keep Our Playground Clean!"

Citizenship
Have students choose a polluted site and make a poster to promote ways of cleaning up the pollution.

Writing
Have students write a letter to their state's department of natural resources or conservation. They should ask questions about the natural resources of the state and problems with pollution.

Unit Summary American Indians came to America long ago. They used the available resources to meet their basic needs. When the Pilgrims and other groups arrived, the American Indians helped them survive by showing them how to grow and hunt food in the new land. The first Thanksgiving was a celebration of the Pilgrims' prosperous harvest. Americans today still celebrate Thanksgiving and other days honoring people and events from our history.

Before Reading the Unit Show students a picture of an unpeopled wilderness landscape. Ask students to imagine that they must live on this land. Ask them how they will survive. Remind students of their three basic needs (food, clothing, and shelter). Ask students to name the ways in which they might meet these needs on this land. Explain to students that this is the situation that faced American Indians and the Europeans who came to America.

Have students read the unit opener and discuss the photograph. Explain that the American Indian woman in the photo is weaving. Weaving is part of her group's culture. Tell students to read the opener questions. Urge them to look for the answers as they read Unit 5.

Point out the Unit Project that students will be working on. Remind them to look for the Project Tips as they read each chapter.

Unit Project

Setting Up the Project Brainstorm a list of holidays with students to get them started. When teams are ready to select a holiday to work on, encourage them to include ways the holiday may be celebrated by people with different cultural traditions. Monitor selections so that a variety of holidays are represented.

Presenting the Project One alternative possibility is to incorporate their pictures into a bulletin-board display. Each team can add decorations and create a display that celebrates their particular holiday.

After Reading the Unit Prompt discussion by asking more questions. Why did the Pilgrims need help from American Indians? Why do families celebrate holidays?

Skill Builder

Reading a Chart

As students read page 104, remind them that a chart makes facts easy to find and understand. Review the skill of reading a chart. As an example, point out the column heads. Then tell students that under the head "Holiday" they can look down and find all holidays listed. By looking along the row for a specific holiday, they can find what is celebrated and when.

Answers: 1. April **2.** Presidents' Day **3.** Answers will vary.

Bibliography

Teacher

Hoven-Severson, L. *Connecting Geography to Literature.* Teacher Created Materials, Inc., 1992.

Low, Alice (compiler). *The Family Read-Aloud Holiday Treasury.* Little Brown, 1991.

National Geographic Society. *Story of America.* National Geographic Society, 1992.

Singleton, L. *G Is for Geography: Children's Literature and the Five Themes.* Science Education Consortium, 1993.

Student

Celsi, Teresa. *Squanto and the First Thanksgiving.* (Real Reading Series) Steck-Vaughn, 1992. (Grade 2)

Chin, Steven A. *Dragon Parade: A Chinese New Year Story.* Steck-Vaughn, 1993. (Grade 2)

Nielsen, Shelly. *Celebrating Independence Day.* (Holiday Celebrations Series) Steck-Vaughn, 1992. (Grades 1–3)

Spencer, Eve. *A Flag for Our Country.* (Stories of America Series) Steck-Vaughn, 1992. (Grade 2)

Stamper, Judith Bauer. *New Friends in a New Land: A Thanksgiving Story.* (Stories of America Series) Steck-Vaughn, 1993. (Grade 2)

Teacher's Resource Binder

Blackline Masters for Unit 5: Unit 5 Project Organizer, Unit 5 Review, Unit 5 Test; Activities for Chapters 10, 11, 12; Outline Map of the United States

Chapter Summary American Indians learned to build their homes from things they found in the places where they lived. They hunted, fished, and grew food. They made all the things they needed for survival.

Chapter Objectives Students will learn to

- identify some American Indian groups.

- tell how the early American Indians found food, built homes, and made clothes.

- identify how parents taught children important survival skills.

- tell how the American Indians used local resources to meet their basic needs.

Vocabulary

tepees, p. 89

Vocabulary Activities Show students a picture of a tepee. Ask students how American Indians used tepees. Point out that not all American Indians lived in tepees. Explain to students that the tepee was used by the Plains Indians as a shelter. Tepees used by the Plains Indians were made out of buffalo skin and could be folded up and easily moved from place to place. Because Plains Indians hunted and followed buffalo herds, having a portable place to live was important. Ask students if they can think a type of shelter we use today that can be moved from place to place. Help students understand that tents are similar to tepees.

Before Reading the Chapter Explain that American Indians lived in the Americas long, long ago. They hunted for food, caught fish, and farmed. Just like children today, early American Indian children loved to play games. The games American Indians played helped boys and girls develop strength and skills. Some games helped prepare boys to become warriors. Games varied according to where groups lived. In the Southwest, foot races were popular. Some race courses were 30 miles long. In the North, a game called Snow Snake was popular. In this game, people competed to slide a spear the greatest distance on ice or snow.

Teaching Suggestions and Answers
Page 87

Have students look at the picture, and explain that the girl and her grandmother are Navajo. This is a group of American Indians who live in the southwestern part of the United States. On a United States map, show students the area of northern New Mexico and Arizona where many Navajo live. Discuss how American Indians pass on their knowledge and skill from generation to generation. Explain that weaving is a skill that Navajo parents and grandparents continue to pass on to their children. American Indians of long ago passed on many important skills, such as hunting, fishing, growing and finding food, building shelters, making clothing, building fires, and so on. Explain that these were skills they needed in order to survive. Invite students to tell about skills their parents or grandparents have taught them. **Students should respond to the question on the page by writing** *her grandmother.*

Page 88

Discuss with students how families of today get food and clothing. Explain that most families buy these and other things they need. However, some families do grow some of their food, make some of their clothing, and make many other things they need. Emphasize, however, that American Indians found, made, or grew almost everything they needed or wanted. For example, the Plains Indians relied on buffaloes for food, clothing, and shelter. Discuss the illustrations with students. Help them identify the tasks shown in each. **Students should put a checkmark on the picture of American Indians planting food. They should put an X on the illustration of the American Indians fishing.**

Page 89

Ask students why they think people sometimes need to work together. Lead them to understand that some jobs are too big for one person. Some jobs can be completed more quickly when several people work together. Call students' attention to the picture and explain that these homes are called tepees. They were made out of animal hides by various groups of American Indians who lived in the midwestern and western areas of the country. Use the illustration to review relative location. **Students should put an *X* on the tepees that are far away. They should put a checkmark on the tepee that is at the far left.**

Project Tip
Discuss the Project Tip with students. Invite them to write their guesses on a piece of paper. Tell them they will learn the answer in a later chapter.

Page 90

Did You Know? Have students look at the pictures of the dwellings shown on this page. Explain that these represent a few of the many kinds of shelters American Indians built. Stress to students that different groups built different shelters based on the resources available in their area and the kind of homes they needed. For example, some places had many buffalo and few trees, so the people built tepees. In other places, there were great forests, and people built homes of wood. You might also explain that American Indians in different places needed protection from different kinds of weather. This need affected their choices of building materials and structure. You might also display some pictures or photographs of pueblos. Pueblos were built by people who lived in a desert environment and needed protection from extreme heat and cold. Pueblos are excellent shelter against heat and cold, but do not give good protection from rain. This is not a problem, since the desert gets little rain. Before students begin their drawings, discuss the resources in your area. What was available to the American Indians of your area that could be used to build a home? Encourage students to think about the materials they could use and how the homes might be built. **Students should draw a picture of a home they might build if it were long ago.**

Page 91

Chapter Checkup Make sure students understand what the correct answers are to the numbered questions.

Answers: Students should circle the following sentences: *The first Americans were American Indians; American Indians made their clothes; American Indians hunted animals for food.* Some American Indians farmed. Ask students to share

their answers. Answers will vary, but student answers should reflect an understanding that all families are alike in many ways: they live, work, and play together. Parents and grandparents teach their children.

After Reading the Chapter

Tell students that various American Indian groups had their own languages. When members of one group wanted to speak to another group, they sometimes used sign language. For example, clasped hands indicated peace, and crossed index fingers signified "tepee." Challenge students to create their own sign language and to use it to communicate with one another. They might develop signs for hunger, welcome, friendship, and so on.

Art
Have students use library resources to learn about tools used by American Indians. Have them draw pictures of some tools and tell the class about them.

Reading
Provide students with some books containing American Indian stories and legends. Have them learn a story. Hold a storytelling event.

Writing
Challenge students to imagine that they are American Indians living long ago. Have them think about what they might do during the course of a day. Ask them to write a description of their day.

Chapter Summary Pilgrims came to America long ago. American Indians helped the Pilgrims succeed by teaching them about hunting, fishing, and growing food in this new land. The Pilgrims and American Indians shared the first Thanksgiving in celebration. People still enjoy this holiday each November, although it is celebrated somewhat differently today.

Chapter Objectives Students will learn to

• identify who celebrated the first Thanksgiving.

• explain how the food was acquired for the feast.

• describe the different ways families celebrate today.

• read a chart.

Vocabulary
chart, p. 94

Vocabulary Activities Write the word *chart* on the board, and read the word to the students. Ask if anyone can tell what the word means. Model sentences using the word. For example, facts can be organized using a chart.

Before Reading the Chapter Display pictures of the settlement at Plymouth. Discuss the homes and the materials used to build them. Ask students where they think the Pilgrims found the wood and the stone to build their homes. Ask students to think about what it would be like to move to a new place. How could they help someone feel more at home in their new community? List the ways on the chalkboard. Tell students that, as they read, they will find out how the American Indians helped the Pilgrims survive in their new land.

Teaching Suggestions and Answers
Page 92
Ask students how the Pilgrims got their food. Explain that they had lived a different kind of life in Europe and were not prepared to have to hunt or grow all their food. The land, animals, and climate were different from those in England. They had to learn new skills, and the American Indians helped teach them these skills. Ask students to look closely at the picture of the first Thanksgiving. Have students describe how the Pilgrims and American Indians are dressed. You might point out to students that the clothes worn by the American Indians were probably made out of deerskin, while the clothes worn by the Pilgrims were probably made from cloth brought from Europe. **Students should write one thing that is happening in the picture. Possible answers: people are cooking, eating, playing, talking.**

Page 93
Discuss the foods served at the first Thanksgiving dinner, explaining that the Pilgrims ate foods such as deer, eels, clams, nuts, corn, berries, and succotash. Invite students to tell about their family Thanksgiving traditions. What foods does your family prepare? Who cooks? Who shares Thanksgiving with your family? At what time of the day does your family eat? Encourage students to share details of any ethnic dishes or traditions that are part of their holiday. **Students should write about their Thanksgiving. Answers will vary.**

You might show students a November calendar and tell them that Thanksgiving is celebrated in the United States on the fourth Thursday of November. Tell them that Thanksgiving also is celebrated in Canada, but it occurs on the second Monday of October in that country. Ask students why they think this holiday is called Thanksgiving. Then explain that the Pilgrims had much to be thankful for: After nearly starving the first year in America, they were now enjoying a large harvest and plentiful amounts of food. Ask students why they think we still celebrate Thanksgiving.

Project Tip
Have students respond to the question in the Project Tip as a class. Invite students either to draw Thanksgiving the way they celebrate it with their families or to draw it the way some other family or group of people celebrates it.

Page 94

Explain to students how to read the chart. Discuss the different categories shown along the top column and side rows. Guide students in using the chart to compare and contrast the first Thanksgiving with Thanksgiving today. Elicit that the two Thanksgivings are alike because turkey is eaten at the meal and many people share the meal. They are different because today Thanksgiving lasts only one day and we buy our turkey at the store. **Students should respond that the first Thanksgiving lasted three days. They should respond that today people buy turkeys in a store.** Explain to students that the first Thanksgiving actually lasted three days. The Pilgrims and American Indians spent the days feasting, dancing, and playing games.

Page 95

Special People Remind students that the Pilgrims had never been to America and did not know the land and weather. The American Indians, and in particular, Squanto, taught the Pilgrims the things they needed to know. Explain that Squanto was especially helpful because he knew English. Several years before the Pilgrims came to America, Squanto had been captured by a ship captain and taken to Spain as a slave. From there he went to England, where he learned English. Later, he returned to America. He was later taken to Plymouth, where he helped the Pilgrims. **Students should write what they think would have become of the Pilgrims without Squanto's help. Possible answer: The Pilgrims might have starved. Student should draw a picture of Squanto helping the Pilgrims.**

Page 96

Chapter Checkup Make sure all students understand what the correct answers are to the questions.

Answers: Students should circle the following true statements: *Squanto helped the Pilgrims; The Pilgrims hunted their turkeys; Pilgrims and American Indians shared the first Thanksgiving.* Ask students to share their answers. Most will say that the Pilgrims invited the American Indians to share Thanksgiving with them because they wanted to thank the American Indians for teaching them to hunt, farm, and fish in the new land.

After Reading the Chapter

Have students tell the story about the first Thanksgiving. Guide them to include who was there, what they ate, and how long it lasted. You may wish to tape record these stories.

Writing

Have students pretend that they are among the Pilgrims planning the first Thanksgiving. The Pilgrims have decided to invite their American Indian friends to share the feast, and they want their children to write a welcoming speech. Have students write the speech and then present it to the class. Alternately, students could write and illustrate invitations to the Thanksgiving feast.

Art

Have students draw or paint a picture of the first Thanksgiving. Remind students that the first Thanksgiving lasted three days and that people celebrated by sharing meals, dancing, and playing games. Encourage students to go back and look at the illustration on page 92 if they need additional ideas. Display the art in the classroom.

Chapter Summary Many kinds of holidays are celebrated in the United States. Holidays are celebrated in many ways. The Fourth of July is the birthday of the United States. The flag and the Liberty Bell are symbols of our country.

Chapter Objectives Students will learn to

- identify some different kinds of holidays celebrated in our country.

- identify the American flag as a symbol of our country.

- recognize other symbols of our country.

Vocabulary

holidays, p. 97   celebrate, p. 97

Vocabulary Activities Have students name a few holidays. Write the names of the holidays on the chalkboard. Then ask students what people do on these holidays. Record responses next to each holiday. Explain that the special activities people do on holidays *celebrate,* or honor and remember, that day. Tell students that in this chapter they will learn about how people in our country celebrate different holidays. Direct students who have any trouble with the vocabulary terms to check the glossary.

Before Reading the Chapter Remind students of occasions that are celebrated during the school year. (Thanksgiving, Christmas, Hanukkah, and so on.) Discuss the different ways in which each is celebrated. Arrange a display of patriotic symbols including the United States flag, the Liberty Bell, the Statue of Liberty, and the bald eagle. Discuss these with students and encourage students to tell what they know about them. Tell students that in this chapter they will learn about more symbols of the United States.

Teaching Suggestions and Answers
Page 97
Tell students that Christmas is a religious holiday on which Christians celebrate the birth of Jesus. Hanukkah is a religious holiday on which Jews celebrate the rededication of an ancient temple

in Jerusalem. Kwanzaa is a cultural festival celebrated by many African Americans. Ask students to name all the holidays their families celebrate. Write the holidays on the chalkboard. Invite students to tell how they celebrate some of the holidays. Point out differences in the ways families celebrate the same holidays. Discuss those holidays with which some students may not be familiar. **Students should write the name of one holiday they celebrate with their families.**

Page 98
Have students look at the picture and describe what is going on. Ask them if they have ever watched a Fourth of July parade. Encourage students to tell what it was like. Ask students to tell other things their families do on the Fourth of July. You might tell students that the Fourth of July is officially called Independence Day. Explain that the United States was not always a country. Long ago, parts of it were ruled by Great Britain. Then, on July 4, 1776, people decided they would form their own country and become independent from Great Britain. **Students should write how their families celebrate the Fourth of July. Answers will vary.**

Page 99
Explain to students that the flag is the symbol of the United States. Display the classroom flag for students and allow them time to count the stars and stripes. Ask students: Why do you think there are fifty stars on the flag? (There are fifty states in the United States.) Ask why they think there are thirteen stripes in the flag. Explain that when the United States first formed, there were just thirteen states. Flag Day is celebrated on June 14. This holiday commemorates the day in 1777 that the "Stars and Stripes" was adopted as the official flag of the United States. **Students should write that there are seven red stripes on the flag. They should write that there are six white stripes.**

Page 100
Point out Philadelphia and the state of Pennsylvania on a map of the United States. Explain that the Liberty Bell was rung to

celebrate the adoption of the Declaration of Independence in 1776. It was rung every Independence Day for the next seventy years, until it developed a crack. Tell students that there are many symbols that make people think of the United States. Encourage them to name some. (Some examples include the Liberty Bell, bald eagle, Washington Monument, Constitution, Statue of Liberty, White House, Capitol Building.) **Students should name something in their school that makes them think of the United States. Answers will vary, but might include the flag, pictures of the bald eagle, Liberty Bell, Washington Monument, and so on.**

Project Tip
Discuss with students the suggestion on page 100. You might suggest that students look back at pictures in this chapter and think about ways the Fourth of July is celebrated that were discussed in class.

Page 101

Did You Know? Explain that the flag is very special because it is a symbol of our country. We must handle it with care. We must not step on it or let it drop. When it is put away, it is folded carefully. If possible, show students how a flag is folded or ask a group of scouts from the school to visit the class and demonstrate for students. **Students should correctly number each picture to the correspond with the statements: 1. We raise the flag. 2. We salute the flag. 3. We fold the flag.**

Page 102

Around the Globe Emphasize that families all over the world celebrate holidays, but that their holidays may be different from ours. Discuss some of the various ways that people celebrate holidays. To illustrate, point out the photograph of the dancers. Tell students that this photograph shows a Mexican fiesta. *Fiesta* is a Spanish word that means "celebration." People dance, play games, dress in colorful clothes and costumes, and eat special foods at fiestas. Tell students that the bottom photograph shows a Swedish celebration on the first day of May. Explain that May Day, which is celebrated in many countries, is a celebration of spring. Call attention to the special costumes and to the green vines decorating the wagon. Encourage

students to tell about other celebrations they may have attended with their families. Examples might include Cinco de Mayo, Greek Independence Day, Chinese New Year, Italian feasts, and so on. **Students should list some holidays their family celebrates. Lists will vary.**

Page 103
Chapter Checkup Make sure all students understand what the correct answers are to the numbered questions.

Answers: Students should circle *red, white,* and *blue;* they should circle *Fourth of July;* they should circle *yes;* they should write *the United States.* Encourage students to share their answers with the class. Possible answers: picnics, dinners, parades, candles.

After Reading the Chapter
Have students make patriotic symbols. They can draw and color the United States flag, a bald eagle, the Liberty Bell, and other symbols.

Writing
Have students write, decorate, and send invitations to people born in other countries, inviting them to visit the class and tell about their holidays.

Social Studies
Have students talk to their parents or to an adult neighbor or relative to learn about a holiday that is celebrated in another culture. Have students write a description of the holiday.

UNIT 1
Letter to Families

Date _____

Dear Family:

Throughout this school year, your child will be studying the family by using the book *Homes and Families*. This book is divided into five units. The first unit, which we are now completing, introduces the family as a group of people who live together and look after each other.

You can help reinforce what we have studied by encouraging your child to talk to you about what we have done. You might even ask your child to read aloud for you a page or two of the unit or to show you some of the pictures.

Listed below are several additional activities you might want to consider doing with your child to support the study of this unit.

Thank you for your interest and support.

Sincerely,

_____

Family Tree

Draw a family tree or put together a family photo album. Tell your child about close and distant family members.

All About Me

Help your child make a scrapbook of things he or she can do well, of activities he or she enjoys, and of family members. Your child might illustrate each category with drawings or with pictures cut from magazines.

Safety First

Review rules for staying safe around your home. These may include rules about where to play, not talking to strangers, and not touching dangerous household cleaners or appliances.

© 1997 Steck-Vaughn Company. *Steck-Vaughn Social Studies: Homes and Families*

Fecha _____

Estimada familia:

Durante este año escolar, su hijo o hija usará el libro *Homes and Families* para estudiar la familia. El libro está dividido en cinco unidades. Ya casi hemos terminado la primera unidad, la cual describe a la familia como un grupo de personas que viven juntas y que se protegen las unas a las otras.

Para ayudar a su hijo o hija a reforzar en casa lo que estamos estudiando en la escuela, anímelo a conversar acerca de lo que estamos haciendo. Incluso le puede pedir que le lea en voz alta una o dos páginas de la unidad, o que le enseñe algunas de las ilustraciones.

A continuación encontrará varias actividades adicionales para hacer con su hijo o hija, que le pueden ayudar a ampliar el estudio de esta unidad.

Muchas gracias por su interés y su apoyo.

Atentamente,

_____

El árbol genealógico

Dibujen juntos un árbol genealógico o preparen un álbum de la familia. Háblele a su hijo o hija acerca de sus parientes cercanos y lejanos.

Así soy yo

Ayude a su hijo o hija a preparar un álbum que incluya recortes de las cosas que él o ella sabe hacer bien, de actividades que le gustan hacer y de miembros de la familia. Su hijo o hija puede ilustrar cada categoría con dibujos o figuras recortadas de revistas.

Seguridad ante todo

Repase las reglas de seguridad para su hogar. Las reglas pueden incluir, por ejemplo, reglas sobre dónde jugar, reglas de comportamiento ante personas extrañas y del manejo de electrodomésticos y líquidos de limpieza.

Date _____

Dear Family:

Your child continues to learn about families as we study Unit 2 of *Homes and Families*. In this unit, we studied how all families have needs and wants. Your child learned that families obtain these needs and wants by working and earning money. Even then, however, families cannot buy everything they need and want; they must make choices. Your child learned why and how families make certain choices.

You can help your child understand and remember this material by encouraging him or her to tell you about the ideas we have studied in this unit. Invite questions about the work you and other family members and neighbors do. Discuss some of the choices your family makes in deciding on food, clothing, and where to live.

In addition, you may want to consider working on one or more of the following activities with your child.

Thank you for your interest and support.

Sincerely,

_____

Shopping List

Have your child go through supermarket ads and circle in one color the foods your family needs. Have your child circle in another color the foods that he or she wants.

What to Wear?

Help your child make a poster to show clothes we need. Divide a large piece of paper into three columns headed: When It Is Warm, When It Is Cold, and When It Is Wet. Let your child cut out pictures of clothing from a magazine or catalog and paste them in the appropriate column.

Homes

As you walk or drive through your community, discuss the many different kinds of homes you see (single-family homes, trailers, apartment buildings, and so on.) Help your child keep a tally so he or she can draw some conclusions about the kinds of homes available in your community.

© 1997 Steck-Vaughn Company. *Steck-Vaughn Social Studies: Homes and Families*

Fecha _____

Estimada familia:

Mientras estudiamos la Unidad 2 de *Homes and Families,* su hijo o hija continúa aprendiendo acerca de las familias en general. En esta unidad aprendimos que todas las familias tienen necesidades y preferencias y que las familias trabajan y ganan dinero para conseguirlas. Sin embargo, las familias no pueden comprar todo lo que necesitan y quieren; así que tienen que escoger entre ellas. En esta unidad, aprendimos por qué y cómo las familias toman decisiones acerca de lo que más les conviene tener.

Usted puede ayudar a su hijo o hija a comprender y recordar lo que estamos estudiando en la escuela. Para hacerlo, anímelo a conversar con usted sobre los conceptos que hemos estudiado en esta unidad. También pueden conversar acerca del trabajo que hace usted y otros familiares y vecinos. Conversen sobre las decisiones que toma su familia acerca de la alimentación, vestuario y vivienda.

A continuación hay varias actividades adicionales que puede hacer con su hijo o hija para ampliar el estudio de esta unidad.

Muchas gracias por su interés y su apoyo.

Atentamente,

_____

Una lista de compras

Pida a su hijo o hija que lea algunos anuncios de ofertas de supermercados y que indique con un lápiz los alimentos que su familia necesita. Luego, pídale que indique con un lápiz de otro color los alimentos que le gustaría comprar, pero que no necesitan verdaderamente.

¿Qué me pongo?

Ayude a su hijo o hija a preparar un cartel que muestre lo que necesitamos para vestirnos en diferentes temporadas. Divida un papel grande en tres columnas, con los siguientes títulos: *Cuando hace calor, Cuando hace frío* y *Cuando llueve.* Permita que él o ella recorte ejemplos de ropa de una revista o de un catálogo y que las pegue en las columnas apropiadas.

Viviendas

Converse con su hijo o hija sobre las distintas clases de viviendas que ven mientras pasean a pie o en auto por su comunidad (casas de familia, condominios, bloques de apartamentos, etc.). Ayúdele a llevar la cuenta de lo que ven, para que pueda sacar conclusiones sobre las clases de viviendas que hay en su comunidad.

Letter to Families

Date _____

Dear Family:

Your child is now completing Unit 3 of *Homes and Families*. The emphasis in these chapters is on the places where people live, work, and play and the rules and laws that help people live together. Students have studied their school and the homes, businesses, and other places in their neighborhood. An important aspect of this unit is the introduction of the skill of understanding and reading a map.

You can help your child master this material by discussing the unit with your child. You might ask your child to show you the maps and explain the map key. Ask your child to describe what is happening in the pictures.

Below are several other activities you might want to do with your child. Choose one or more that interest you and your child.

Thank you for your interest and support.

Sincerely,

_____

Tour Your Neighborhood

Go on a walk around your neighborhood with your child and point out various places, such as the fire station, police station, library, and post office as well as shops and the homes of friends.

Simon Says

Play Simon Says using the directional words *near, next to, up, down, top, bottom, over, under, behind, in front of, left,* and *right.* For example, "Simon says to touch the top of your head."

Fecha _____

Estimada familia:

Su hijo o hija está trabajando ahora en la Unidad 3 de *Homes and Families*. En estos capítulos el énfasis está en los lugares donde la gente vive, trabaja y juega, y en las reglas y leyes que ayudan a la gente a vivir en una sociedad. Los estudiantes han aprendido sobre la escuela y las viviendas, los negocios y otros lugares de la comunidad. En esta unidad se introducen las destrezas de la lectura y comprensión de los mapas.

Usted puede conversar sobre el contenido de la unidad con su hijo o hija para ayudarle a comprender este material más a fondo. Puede pedirle que le muestre los mapas que ha estudiado y que le explique la classe de cada uno. También puede pedirle que le explique de lo que ocurre en las ilustraciones.

A continuación hay otras actividades para hacer con su hijo o hija. Escoja una o más actividades que les interese a ambos.

Muchas gracias por su interés y su apoyo.

Atentamente,

_____

Un paseo por el vecindario

Tome una caminata por el vecindario con su hijo o hija y señálele los distintos lugares de importancia en su comunidad, tales como la estación de bomberos, la estación de policía, la biblioteca y la oficina del correo, así como las tiendas y las casas de sus amigos.

Simón dice

Jueguen al juego de "Simón dice", usando las palabras direccionales *cerca de, junto a, arriba de, abajo de, encima de, sobre, detrás de, delante de, al lado de, a la izquierda de* y *a la derecha de.* Por ejemplo: "Simón dice que te toques la parte de arriba de la cabeza".

Date _____

Dear Family:

Your child is now completing Unit 4 of *Homes and Families*. In this unit, we are reading about Earth and different kinds of places on Earth, such as mountains, flat land, and rivers. We are also studying the resources on Earth that provide families with the things they need and want. In one chapter, we are learning about how these resources can be destroyed by pollution and how people can stop pollution and protect these resources.

To help reinforce your child's understanding of this material, encourage your child to read some of the material to you and to explain the projects our class is working on.

Listed below are some additional activities. Consider doing one of them with your child.

Sincerely,

_____

Family Travel

Tell your child about places your family has lived or visited. Describe the mountains, hills, rivers, and other features of these places. If you have photographs, show them to your child to help him or her visualize the different kinds of land on Earth.

Litter Patrol

As you go shopping or to other places in the community, call your child's attention to different kinds of pollution, such as litter, smog, polluted water, industrial waste, and so on. Consider helping your child pick up litter near your home or in the park. You may even want to work with some neighbors to organize a neighborhood cleanup.

Natural Resources in the Community

As you walk or drive through your community, discuss with your child the natural resources you see. Point out that trees, lakes, rivers, and even soil are natural resources. Encourage your child to tell how people use these resources and how people can conserve and keep clean your community's natural resources.

Fecha _____

Estimada familia:

Ahora su hijo o hija está completando la Unidad 4 de *Homes and Families*. En esta unidad estamos leyendo sobre la Tierra y los distintos fenómenos naturales que ocurren en ella, tales como las montañas, los valles y los ríos. También estamos estudiando nuestro planeta y sus recursos, los cuales proporcionan a las familias lo que necesitan y desean. En uno de los capítulos, aprendemos cómo estos recursos pueden ser destruidos por la polución y cómo la gente puede detener la polución para proteger estos recursos.

Usted puede ayudar a su hijo o hija a reforzar en casa la comprensión de lo que ha aprendido en la escuela. Para hacerlo, anímelo a leerle en voz alta algunas páginas del material. También le puede pedir que le explique los proyectos en los que la clase está trabajando.

A continuación hay varias actividades adicionales. Considere trabajar en una de ellas con su hijo o hija.

Atentamente,

_____

Un viaje en familia

Converse con su hijo o hija sobre los lugares donde su familia ha vivido o lugares que la familia ha visitado. Descríbale las montañas, las colinas, los ríos y otras características de dichos lugares. Si tiene fotografías de esos lugares, muéstreselas a su hijo o hija para que vean las distintas clases de terrenos que existen.

La patrulla de la basura

Cuando vayan de compras o visiten otros lugares de la comunidad, llame la atención de su hijo o hija a distintas clases de polución, tales como la basura, el smog, el agua contaminada, los deshechos industriales, etc. Si es posible, ayúdele a recoger la basura que está cerca de su casa o en el parque. También puede trabajar con algunos de los vecinos para organizar un grupo de limpieza del vecindario.

Los recursos naturales de la comunidad

Mientras caminan o manejan por su vecindario, converse con su hijo o hija sobre los recursos naturales que hay en su comunidad. Indíquele que los árboles, los lagos, los ríos y aun la tierra misma, son todos recursos naturales. Anime a su hijo o hija a decirle cómo usan las personas estos recursos y cómo pueden conservar y mantener limpios los recursos naturales de la comunidad.

Date _____

Dear Family:

    Your child is now completing the final unit of *Homes and Families*. This unit introduced American Indians and told how they lived in America. It explained that much later Pilgrims came to America and celebrated the first Thanksgiving with the American Indians. Your child has learned about Thanksgiving and some of the other holidays that people celebrate.

    You can help reinforce your child's understanding of the unit by looking at the pictures and discussing the holidays depicted. Talk to your child about the holidays your family celebrates and explain what these holidays mean to your family.

    Below are several additional activities you might want to consider doing with your child to support our study of this unit.

    Thank you for your interest and support.

Sincerely,

_____

Helping Out

    When you are planning a family celebration, let your child help by listing the jobs that need to be done. Then give your child responsibility for seeing that some job gets done.

Holiday Traditions

    If your family friends or neighbors celebrate different holidays than your family celebrates, or celebrate them in different ways, invite them to tell your child about the holidays. You may want to ask them to join your family for a holiday and to share traditions.

© 1997 Steck-Vaughn Company. *Steck-Vaughn Social Studies: Homes and Families*

Fecha _____

Estimada familia:

Su hijo o hija está completando la última unidad de *Homes and Families*. Esta unidad presenta a los indígenas americanos y cuenta cómo vivían en América del Norte antes de la llegada de los europeos. La unidad describe la llegada de los peregrinos y la celebración de la primera fiesta de Acción de Gracias. Además de esa celebración, los estudiantes aprenden acerca de algunas otras fiestas que celebra la gente.

Usted puede ayudar a su hijo o hija a reforzar en casa la comprensión de la unidad que estamos estudiando en la escuela. Para hacerlo, observen juntos las ilustraciones de la unidad en el libro de texto y conversen sobre las fiestas que aparecen allí. Conversen acerca de las fiestas que celebran en familia y de lo que significan esas fiestas para su familia.

A continuación aparecen varias actividades adicionales para hacer con su hijo o hija, que le ayudarán en el estudio de la unidad.

Gracias por su interés y su apoyo.

Atentamente,

_____

Vamos a ayudar

Cuando estén planeando una celebración en familia, permita que su hijo o hija ayude a preparar una lista de todas las cosas que se necesitan llevar a cabo. Luego dele la responsabilidad de completar algunas de esas cosas.

Fiestas tradicionales

Si algunos amigos de la familia o vecinos celebran distintas fiestas de las que celebra su propia familia, o si las celebran de distintas maneras, invítelos a contarle a su hijo o hija las maneras en que ellos celebran dichas fiestas. Puede invitarlos a participar con su familia en una fiesta especial para compartir sus tradiciones.

Name _____

© 1997 Steck-Vaughn Company. *Steck-Vaughn Social Studies: Homes and Families*